AT HOME IN BALI

Photographs by
ISABELLA GINANNESCHI

Text by
MADE WIJAYA

ABBEVILLE PRESS PUBLISHERS
New York   London   Paris

CONTENTS

THE GOOD LIFE

BEING AT HOME IN BALI is being in love with nature and, if you're lucky, with your fellow courtyard inhabitants. It is the feeling of security, if you are Balinese, that your ancestral spirits are all lined up and keeping an eye on you from their perch. And it is the feeling of luxury, if you're an expatriate, that there's always someone to roll out the mat and water the garden.

In Bali one doesn't go home and shut out the world. Home is not a cocoon but a microcosm—the Balinese call it Buana Alit, "the small world"—of the greater world outside with its myriad influences and strata. The front door is always open in a Balinese house, and the spirit of the house is always entwined with the spirits of the universe. Even without the requisite shrines to the spirit of the land and the altar to the sun god, one senses, from the offerings placed everywhere and the abundant beauty in nearly all Balinese homes—be they ethnic chic or kitsch—that house pride is a big factor in the Balinese lifestyle.

The typical Balinese house is ordered to the Hindu Balinese universe; the kitchen, for example, is usually in the southern part of the house, under Brahma, the god of fire, and the family house temple is always in the propitious northeastern corner of the compound, nearest the holy Mount Agung and the eastern sphere of Lord Shiva, the supreme deity. Even foreigners' homes must have shrines because the spirit of the land belongs to the landlord, not the tenant.

There is a sense of romance and mystery that goes with being at home in Bali; the courtyard garden is traditionally dimly lit; the palm leaves sway against a starlit sky. The ripple of gamelan music is often heard picking through the dense foliage; the air is muggy and thick. Nocturnal shadows flicker against pavilion walls; the slightly spooky silhouettes of statues and shrines add a sense of magic to the pervading atmosphere of the exotic, and the Oriental.

The very name *Bali* conjures up visions of the exotic—and intimations of the world's most gorgeous culture. Once on the island one is impressed by the diversity—the way the geography changes from coastal to alpine in the course of a short drive, the way the mood changes from urban guerrilla to monastic mellow in the course of an hour—and the dynamic nature of the Balinese building industry. Here "new is holy," and heaven help anyone who stands in the way of the wrecker's ball! Everyone is forever building, embellishing, frosting, carving, and gardening—"far too much creative endeavor," was the summation of the greatest embellisher of our era, Noël Coward.

Traditional Balinese architecture has Javanese, Chinese, and South Indian elements, all laid over a strong ancient Indonesian/Polynesian base—the Balinese love to absorb, adopt, and adapt. The simple longhouses and terraced sanctuaries of the ancient pre-Hindu Balinese have become highly stylized hybrids of both Hindu and Chinese parentage.

Simple beach huts evolved over centuries of "colonization by contagion" into handsome pavilions after the South Indian and Sri Lankan model. From the sixteenth century on, various colonial influences—Portuguese and Dutch in particular—have swept across the fertile architectural "plain." For instance, the

so-called *pesisir* style—seen in the whitewashed walls and colonial architecture of certain coastal villages—survives today as testimony to the influence of early European merchants involved in the spice trade. From the days of the first trading vessel—the Dutch expedition to the East Indies led by Van Houtman in 1650, when two sailors jumped ship and settled in East Bali for twenty-five years—European models for bathrooms and kitchens in particular have been added to the vocabulary of domestic architecture. With the various Portuguese, English, and finally Dutch administrations came various styles. In Jakarta, Indonesia's capital, we still find high-windowed town houses after the Lisbon model. In Banda, in the Spice Islands, we find Georgian *parkeneers'* (plantation owners') bungalows from the era of colonial exploitation. The Bali Hotel in Denpasar and the Narmada Hotel in Sanur survive today as fine examples of Dutch Colonial Art Deco, from the period preceding independence. All these models have influenced local architects and designers to the present day.

Before delving into the details of form and function and style, one should know that Bali has been the end of the road for cultural and artistic migrations for many thousands of years. The ancient proto-Malays, who brought wet rice cultivation from the tropical reaches of present-day Laos, Myanmar, and Yunnan, seem to have ceased their eastward migration in Bali and deposited some of their greatest cultural treasures here. The spread of Islam in medieval times also stopped at Bali when the priests and princes from Java's greatest Hindu empire migrated here, bringing with them more veils of sophistication and philosophy to lay over their eager host. With this slow migration came redbrick temple gates, the giant pavilions of Javanese palaces, and the many palettes of court colors. The notion of garden follies done on a grand scale was also imported at this time.

Geographically, Bali is the end of Asia: Wallace's line, which runs between Bali and Lombok, the neighboring island to the east, was postulated by British naturalist Alfred Russel Wallace to separate Asian from Austronesian flora and fauna—a line declaring "the wombat starts here." And wombats there have been.

In the 1970s, with the arrival of mass tourism and the various day-feeding marsupials from Down Under, ballet dancers started leaving their stages for a life here on juice blenders. The cultural dilution was not as great, however, as in Hawaii or Acapulco—the Balinese culture has, over the centuries, resisted colonialization and Islamization and come through relatively intact. Terms like *turis, art shop,* and *losmen* (hostel) may be here to stay—in fact, today's hotels are considered New Age temples to architectural prowess—but the richness and resilience of the Balinese culture is proving to be the island's saving grace.

With mass tourism came mass investment, a feeding frenzy of investors from Jakarta and Singapore, two regional capitals known for hard-nosed urban attitudes. Their influence on the architectural language of Bali's tourist hubs bore much fancy fruit—the Ghost-Train Gothic school of "Balinaise" wedding-cake architecture, with its neocolonial bonsai gardens, to name just one. The arrival of the hippies, surfies, New Agers, and late-ly, Zen yuppies, by contrast, fueled various building booms, like the Rustic Charm movement, the Expatriate Dream Home movement, the *aman*-wannabe, and the po-mo-for-homo. One can't help getting excited writing about the Balinese lifestyle, be it indigenous or adopted, because it is always so weird and wonderful. *Fertile, fecund,* and *fanciful* are certainly three words that sum up the state of Balinese architecture today.

Foreigners come and fall in love with the island, the culture, and the people, and want to build an homage to that love. The fiercely industrious Balinese then want to keep up with the foreigners, who are themselves busy going native. The hotels may be the New Age temples, but the many temples are being rebuilt in finishes kept alive by the hotel industry.

This book will lead you through various facets of the Balinese experience, through the dwellings of Bali's inhabitants. Generously interspliced are images of the Balinese way of living—the vibrant customs and religious practices and the colorful patterns of day-to-day life.

ABOVE: GARLAND'S SIGNATURE
LOUNGE SET—BLACK BAMBOO
IN A VALLEY VIEW.

RIGHT: THE ESTATE IS
FOREVER REWARDING, WITH
INTRIGUING SHADOWS AND
STARTLING VISTAS.

OPPOSITE: THE TORAJAU RICE
STORAGE PAVILION, WHICH
CAME AS PART OF GARLAND'S
DOWRY WHEN SHE MARRIED
AMIR RABIK OF SANYYINGAN.

dramatic alpine scenery, planting baby lettuce in the lava dust.

Linda's rise to design prominence started in the village of Pengosekan, about three miles (5 km) from her present river valley home. There she developed lines of creative housewares—carved and colored miniature trees and banana leaf trays to start—that influenced the world's souvenir and housewares market in a big way. Today in Martinique, Malibu, Mozambique, and Madras you will find Linda Garland–derivative souvenir items still on the best-seller shelves.

After a successful partnership with Dewa Nyoman Batuan's Community of Artists, who she helped train, Linda moved up the hill to Central Ubud, her second Bali home, and started, with Belinda, Lady Montagu, a range of very successful embroi-

dered linen to add to her already extensive textile range. She loaned her eye and taste to a successful collection of neocolonial furniture in the United States in 1994, having previously championed the bamboo sofa and beaded poufs that came to the forefront of yuppie chic. Her "Ethnic Chic" interior designs for Richard Branson, David Bowie, and Japanese contracting tycoon Kajima were all much published and admired.

Her first *petit palais,* a series of trad-mod bungalows overlooking the rice fields near Ubud, was a testing ground for her nascent design ideas and those of her husband, designer Amir Rabik. It was a great success and attracted a lot of attention.

Linda's present Bali estate, at Nyuh Kuning, a rural village in the ravishing countryside south of Ubud, is a nesting ground

ABOVE: Up in a belvedere, a welcoming planter's chair.

LEFT: Many pavilions on the estate are open to the sumptuous grounds.

BELOW: A woven bamboo screen doubles as towel rack.

OPPOSITE: Hammocks are a big part of the Garland estate lifestyle.

for all her creative ideas and aspirations. She lives in the "real" Bali, the Bali of mountain walks, home grown spices and sisterly servants. Spread over an idyllic river valley are four bungalows and one main pavilion, as well as numerous garden pavilions, both practical and poetic. Her outhouses are like garden kiosks rising along paths of botanical garden splendor. The estate is more palm grove and wild grassland than garden, more hacienda than house, with its grassy terraces and river boulder waterfalls. A forest of bamboo stands on the opposite bank, and her land is home to her burgeoning collection of rare and important bamboo specimen plants.

The estate has grown houses and offices as Linda gathered apostles and gained prominence on the international green scene. Bamboo (its versatility and its beauty) is Linda's main cause, and it is also the theme of every structure and many of the loose furnishings in the home.

From these inspiring surroundings Linda continues to inspire: the Edwardian butterfly hunter among her medals, her handmaidens ascurry. The tropical world awaits her next epoch-defining move. Her deft decorative touch (spacious, stylish, original) is everywhere evident, particularly in the use of Indo-

OPPOSITE: A JAVO-COLONIAL TEAK BENCH, WITH CUSHIONS UPHOLSTERED IN THE DISTINCTIVE CIREBON CLOUD PATTERN, ON A LOWER GARDEN TERRACE.

LEFT: BAMBOO AND FERN LEAF IMPRINTS ON A CONCRETE FLOOR TILE.

RIGHT: THE BAMBOO-SHINGLED ROOF OF THE POOL PAVILION PROVIDES A CRISP ACCENT AMID THE VERDANT FOLIAGE.

nesian textiles and textile motifs. She has always stretched the boundaries of creativity.

Party time at the Garland estate means high style at the old corral: Linda combines stellar guests with sensational food—Balinese and Santa Fe fusion—and a trademark magical ambience.

Pleasure palace, parkland retreat, party planetarium, suffragette's soup kitchen . . . the Irish wonder woman's inspiring house is proof that the price for peace is eternal vigilance!

LEFT: ALL OF THE BEDS IN THE HOUSE ARE COZY NOOKS FEATURING GARLAND'S HANDSOME WHITE-ON-WHITE EMBROIDERED TEXTILES.

ABOVE: THE JUNGLE POOL, LINED WITH RIVER BOULDERS.

RIGHT: A PIECE FROM GARLAND'S SIGNATURE FURNITURE RANGE. IN THE BACKGROUND, A DELICATELY CARVED PAVILION FRONT IN THE KUDUS STYLE, FROM EAST JAVA.

OPPOSITE: THE CLASSIC ENGLISH COLONIAL SETTING: A COMFY ARMCHAIR, WELL PADDED, IN DAPPLED LIGHT. POSITIONED HERE, IT POINTS LIKE A SHEEPDOG TO A FAVORITE VIEW.

ADOBE ABODE:
A RUSTIC MASTERPIECE
ON THE RIDGE

JOHN AND CYNTHIA HARDY'S LOW–TECH MARVEL AT SAYAN has been called part Flintstone, part Waterworld. Its distinctive look—mountain cabin with stretched membrane flaps—certainly provokes a lot of comment among the locals. Being designers, the Hardys spent a good deal of time looking for a design collaborator before asking Cheong Yew Kuan, a young Malaysian architect based in Bali, to help in the realization of their dream dwelling.

Yew Kuan had previously worked with Kerry Hill Architects on the Amanusa Hotel in South Bali and was passionate about the project from the start. He conceived a rude timber pavilion, like a giant Borneo longhouse, with lots of transparency to cap-

ABOVE: THE PASSAGES BETWEEN THE PAVILION AND THE BOUNDARY WALL ARE LIKE SUBTERRANEAN CAVERNS, PIERCED WITH PATCHES OF SHARP TROPICAL LIGHT.

RIGHT: THE RUSTIC KITCHEN—THE HARDYS FEED SCORES OF WORKERS EVERY DAY.

ture the remarkable view. Mammoth ironwood posts, over twenty-six feet (8 m) long, recycled from telephone poles form the basic structure. Solid *merbau* floorboards cut from old logs, two inches thick, come from Java. *Lebah* tree branches selected in situ by John Hardy and Yew Kuan in Banyuwangi, East Java, were tied and a canvas skin was stretched to form caveman canopies, needed for protection from the sun and rain at the open-air entry points to the building. The ground floor of the two-level structure is a rude mix of gangplanks, packed mud, pebbles, pond, draw bridges, rough-hewn flying buttresses, paved "garden" areas and slate-tiled sitting areas. Jeweler John's fine eye came into play in the crafting of various unique finishes for the structure's walls and windows. Woven bamboo panels were simulated, out of scale, in sand-colored cement, and fixed as wall panels between the free-form columns. Garden walls were sculpted from mud using the packed-mud building tradition, called *popolan,* common in mountain village architecture. Every window latch, washbasin, and curtain rod was turned into a neo–Bronze Age work of art: it is in this detailing that the house rises above the bounds of the original and becomes truly inspired.

Cynthia and John furnished the spaces—more tree house than lodge—with professional help from Hinke Zieck using

OPPOSITE AND ABOVE: THE UNDERSIDE OF THE LONGHOUSE, THE VOID DECK, IS FURNISHED WITH AN ECLECTIC MIX OF JAVANESE PRIMITIVE FURNITURE COLLECTED OVER TWO DECADES OF SCOURING THE ANTIQUE SHOPS OF BALI.

RIGHT: A SINGAPORE TREE AND A "SKIRTING" OF LOTUS LEAVES SOFTEN THE AUSTERE FRONT ELEVATION OF THE LONGHOUSE.

their collection of Javanese "primitive" furniture. As accents they added Balinese doors and shapely artifacts gleaned from twenty years feathering various Balinese nests (this writer remembers John's first humble abode—an adobe hut with a one-tatami veranda in the hills behind Ubud).

Gardenwise, the compound is slightly compromised, the house having broadsided the view and eaten its way to the boundary wall on both sides. A decision was made to keep the garden very simple; inside the entrance gate, grass and pebble terraces "roll through" the transparent architecture and out to embrace the view. This aspect of the compound's design has been a great success: the first impression as one pushes aside the boul-

LEFT: The Hardys' impressive collection of primitive sampan paddles.

RIGHT: Architect Yew Kuan's clever faux woven bamboo plaster wall.

BELOW: Early 20th-century Balinese doors are used as accents throughout the house.

OPPOSITE, TOP: Inspired by Nordic sleigh beds, the massive timber bed is softened by folds of gathered mosquito netting.

OPPOSITE, BOTTOM: A Kohler bathtub in the garden kiosk-like main bathroom.

der at the main gate is a giant house frame silhouetted boldly against the valley view. Beyond the building, valleyside, the Hardys have preserved bamboo groves and native trees—allowing the house to nestle in nature, as it were. Only the pool area is overtly landscape designed, but care has been taken here to use shapes and materials that blend with the environment.

This is by far the most innovative house since painter Walter Spies's 1936 modified *wantilan* (community hall) in Ubud. It is poised to inspire young designers and define a new strand of Balinese architectural design.

ABOVE: THE TENSION-EDGE PLUNGE POOL ON THE VIEW SIDE OF THE VOID DECK CAPTURES IN REFLECTION THE STUNNING RIVER VALLEY VIEW (RIGHT).

LEFT: A DETAIL OF YEW KUAN'S UNIQUE ARCHITECTURE—HERE A STRETCHED WATER BUFFALO HIDE CANOPY—FOR THE JEWELER'S DREAM HOUSE.

MINIMALIST MANSION IN THE MONKEY FOREST

THERE HAS LONG BEEN A LINK BETWEEN THE AUSTRALIAN art world and Bali: many artists retrench to Bali to extend the boundaries of their creativity in the heady artistic atmosphere of the island.

Ceramic artists Philip Lakeman and Graham Oldroyd left Australia in 1993 after completing a fifty-five-yard (50 m) mural for Australia's new Parliament House. They burst onto the Sanur art scene as high-flying ceramists, working closely at first with local manufacturing czars Brent Hesselyn and Ade Waworuntu, of U.D. Jenggala Ceramics fame. Under Jenggala's liberal patronage, the hardworking couple were ushered into the fast lane, where they took off in a blaze of revolutionary new finishes—soon applied to the walls and tables of the rich and famous from their studio, Pesamuan.

Quietly too they did their art pieces; quieter still they built

LEFT: THE MEMPHIS-LOOK ENTRANCE TO THE HOUSE.

ABOVE: A RARE MALAYSIAN DRACAENA PLANT IN A STARK MODERNIST COURT.

33

LEFT: LILY PADS IN FORMATION ON A FORMAL GARDEN POND.

RIGHT: A TIGHTLY COMPOSED CORNER OF THE MAIN LOGGIA WITH ITS COFFERED BALINESE THATCH CEILING.

their "Palazzo Liberazione" high in the hills above the artists' colony of Ubud. It is a fresh breeze in the doldrums of neocolonial, neo-hippie "*aman*-wannabes." God bless them.

"Albert Speer meets Hindu Holiday" is a term I often use to describe the "tombstones to minimalism" that pop up regularly on the architectural scene. Philip and Graham's house is more Cecil B. DeMille than Leni Reifenstahl; it is also more Australian, showing the Australians' love for bright color and sharp design statements.

The entrance is a tad operatic in the daytime (Memphis meets Marilyn Manson): the house is really designed for nighttime entertaining, when the bright young people in bright new (tight) clothes descend like locusts. Everything is clean and simple and uncluttered, with strong planes (vertical and hori-

LEFT: HELICONIAS AND COCONUT PALMS FLOOD A LIVING ROOM VIEW.

OPPOSITE: GRAHAM OLDROYD'S PAINTING, "ICARUS," ABOVE A PRIMITIVE JAVANESE TEAK "RAFFLES" BENCH, LIGHTLY DISTRESSED.

zontal) of color and texture. There are no tricky changes in level or overtly framed views: things become apparent through holes in the architecture, or as one turns a corner. Things are perched, not placed. Surfaces are textured, in neat panels, or left wholesome and undecorated. The jungle is beyond the boundary. Neither landscape nor traditional tricks have been borrowed; but the body and soul of the house are Balinese. This is pavilion style in a Mies van der Rohe way. Plants, where used to lift and separate, are used architecturally, like the *Cordyline australis* ("Bali's own bayonet") and other horticultural marvels that stick up and don't soften.

"Soft" is not an option.

We are, therefore we are hard-edged.

Blue and mustard and burnt sienna bring spark to the stark. French designer Christian Liagre is obviously an influence in the functional art.

The house is a gallery for Graham's bold canvases and Philip's classy ceramic art.

HIGH STYLE IN THE
HIGHER ALTITUDES

Dutch-Australian painter Ian van Wieringen is the
gentle *grand seigneur* of the fun-loving brat pack that monitors
New Age Bali: all aspirants to mountain sagedom will eventually beat a path to his door. Van has lived on the Sayan "Lover's
Leap," which overlooks the stunning Ayung River Valley, for
more than twenty-five years. His first house was a tiny thatched
hut, built in 1975: it was the first of many incarnations he calls
his "womb rooms" for "incubating art and love trysts." ("You're
the King of the Ridge," a testy town planner once moaned,
"you get all the girls!")

"No vanity" is Van's catchword, and indeed the theme of the
decoration. But a gin and tonic is served by the loving live-in
couple at the gate, and in the hillside lifestyle there is a touch of
the Hugh Hefner, albeit pared down (just one can of smoked
oysters in the fridge these days).

ABOVE: An "up the Khyber pass" view of Van's
personally designed studio home.

RIGHT: The platform under the frangipani tree from where
the "Dancer of the Universe" entertains his many fans.

36

Entering through the house's Balinese mud gate with its creaky bamboo door is to step through Alice's looking glass: the view is but a subtle backdrop to the clever blend of pixie garden and noddy house (slightly cheesy)—noddy and nimble, nature-loving and narcissistic. Van's house exudes art, as do his finger-tips. The line of the garden is expressed in the lines of his vibrant paintings, which in turn affect the lanes of paint bottles and art books that make up the interior of his studio–sitting room. Off this central art factory are niches for cooking, "high cozy" nich-es dug into the hillside below, a niche for his goat named Satay, niches for nooky, and niches for his two children, Tao and Zen (Now and Then).

Van's present house of "womb rooms" is fifth-generation, fully baked "gynecological gorgeous," on an island renowned for its gorgeousness. His cave of carnal delights has grown into a three-storied pagoda of pleasure with a pixie-glen garden of anthropomorphic statuary.

Fern forests, banyan trees, frangipanis, and waterfalls com-plete the seductive picture. The view is not so much in your face as it is there to be nestled into, high up, on a valley-viewing plat-form of bamboo inside the warm embrace of a frangipani tree, itself smothered with orchids and dripping staghorn ferns. Sunset is a sublime experience. Van can be found curled up here almost any hour of the day, save the morning hours, dispensing wisdom and Taoist truths when not working on his "swirling art." He is the self-styled "Dancer of the Universe," and his

house is a ravineside citadel of cosmic consciousness.

As Van often burns the midnight oil, his studio is fully open to the magic embrace of moonlit nights: bedrooms are sequestered in dark niches on the upper floor, for daytime quiet.

Years ago, well ahead of the trend for collecting Javanese "antiques," Van started making murals of furniture bits and pieces—a bed leg here, a chair back there, Louise Nevelson–like—which provide decorative encrustations between the fabulously painted walls and the delicately poised statuary.

There is a Balinese *mandi* bathroom, barely a grotto with a bamboo spout, alive with grotesques by Ubud wizard sculptor Wayan Cemul, and a "Western" bathroom decorated with moon orchids, totem poles, and dadaist jokes. It is *not* a hippie house with Indian tents and piles of musty cushions by any means. The house is a take on "high cozy" in the Dutch-Australian-Balinese-Colonial style, and is also a testament to the basic principle of Balinese life: Art = Love = Nature.

WEEKEND RETREAT:
ROUSSEAU REVISITED

IN 1993 AMERICAN MUSICOLOGIST COLIN MCPHEE BUILT A Balinese house on the edge of the ridge above the magnificent Ayung River Valley.

His house and his life in Bali were celebrated in a wonderful book, *A House in Bali,* which was principally a record of his experiences with Balinese musicians and dancers, and with the life and culture that surrounds the music world. Photos of his house in that book show a series of thatched huts set on a winding path in a bamboo forest.

The McPhee house overlooked a horseshoe meander in a sensuously sculpted river valley. In the distance one glimpsed the giant banyan tree of Bongkasa village (rumored the world's largest at that time), the Nutmeg (Monkey) Forest of Sangeh, and the towering cone of Mount Batu Karo beyond.

LEFT: THE AUTHOR'S OUTDOOR DINING TERRACE
WITH OBJETS (AND PLANTS) TROUVÉS.

ABOVE: ARTIST SHANE SWEENEY'S GARDEN DRINKS
TABLE ON THE OUTDOOR DINING TERRACE.

At dawn, then and now, a curtain of bright light crosses the valley as the sun races over the ridge to Sayan's east, illuminating this spectacle of nature. At sunset flocks of white herons float past one's nose, airborne accents for one of the seven natural wonders of Bali.

When in 1980 I acquired the Colin McPhee land, only the foundations of these houses remained. The view, however, was still magnificent and unspoiled. I slowly set about building Taman Bebek, a series of cottages approximating the scale and layout of the original pavilions, and it became my home from 1985 to 1987. I loved the valley and the gentle people of the neighboring village, Sayan. The ridge had, through the decades, retained the stamp of artist's retreat: painters, writers, dancers, and scholars from all over the world had made the Sayan ridge their home, including

OPPOSITE: KITSCH MATADOR LAMPS FLANK A PETER WRIGHT WATERCOLOR OF SYDNEY HARBOR.

RIGHT: A VIEW FROM THE DRESSING ROOM HIGHLIGHTS AN ART DECO–EGYPTIAN-REVIVAL HALL MIRROR FROM A GOLD SELLER'S SHOP IN WEST SUMATRA.

BOTTOM: STEPHEN LITTLE'S INSPIRED TROMPE L'OEIL TREATMENT FOR A DOOR IN THE SITTING ROOM.

anthropologist Margaret Mead, painter Ian van Wieringen, and French historian-dancer Agnes Montenay.

By 1990, however, the writing was on the wall: the ridge, though still completely charming, was entering its pretourist development phase and was starting to attract a less academic-artistic following. Ghettos of the satay-satiated were springing up on the "dangerously" steep slopes of the river valley immediately below; the local artist colony of Ubud had become a shopping mall. I decided to sell out to the tourist dollar and turn Taman Bebek into a small hotel.

I had long since ceased living in Sayan but still liked to spend the odd weekend there and invite people for a meal in the seductive ambience of the breathtaking rice paddy views. I wanted a new house to showcase the view and was keen to flex some architectural muscle on a neighboring site. With my partners Gusti Sarjana and Nyoman Miyoga I conceived a "presidential villa" in a style that could be called "power dressing." I wanted to do a substantial house that would signal a new direction for traditional Balinese architecture and also show off our architectural office's decorative clout. The land's three gentle terraces were turned into a dramatic two, with a lozenge-shaped lap pool taking up most of the lower terrace. Three traditional

LEFT AND RIGHT: JAVANESE NOBLES (AFTER 9TH-CENTURY GLASS PAINTING ORIGINALS) GUARD THE ENTRANCE TO THE THRONE ROOM.

structures were then built on the sizable upper terrace.

The main house was built in the form of pure Balinese *wantilan*—the two-storied community hall that hosts cockfights in the wet season and gamelan rehearsals in the dry. This building was to house the public areas—the living and dining rooms—with the master bedroom above. A staff house was attached to the kitchen section of the main house off the entrance court. Off the far corner of the wantilan, the valley-view side, we built a "Royal Suite" bedroom inspired by the large *loji* pavilions I had admired in the Saren palace of nearby Ubud. We gave this Royal Suite a "Queenslander" tropical bungalow touch by adding a wide terrace accessed through giant louvered doors. There was little garden left on the upper terraces, so I wanted the interiors to be sparkling: too many valley view houses are drab, I feel, once the view "goes out" at 6:00 P.M. I enlisted the services of trompe l'oeil artist du jour Stephen Little and gave his florid fantasies full rein. The results were miraculous: he made the Royal Suite feel like a cardinal's bedroom in an ancient Portuguese castle. The tile frieze painted up the wall was like the side wall on a Venetian gondola garage, updated in the 1950s. The bedroom had bold character and wit.

In the main house the maestro created frescos taken from our joint past at Port Jackson (Sydney Harbor). On one sliding door Stephen painted, in naive neo-native fashion, a fresco of a fictitious, operatic First Fleet arriving at Padang Bai, the port of East Bali. It had been inspired by a similar work on the stairs of the legendary Taj Hotel in Port Agauarda in Goa, India, a snapshot of which I had provided. Other screens featured hyperreal trompe l'oeil of coconut-weave walls. On the pewter-colored cement floors of the main living room Little painted tarot-card heraldic rugs complete with the corners scuffed up. Harlequin tile patterns, rich wall colors, and high camp decorative touches (Matador lamps astride Javanese rent trolleys) completed the exotic mix.

It is ironic, one local commented, that the house is now occupied by the management of the audacious Four Seasons Resort, Sayan. Now, cocktail parties are held as guests marvel at the Christmas-tree-like lights of the resort. Gone forever are the fireflies and full moon spectacles. But peace reigns.

ABOVE: STEPHEN LITTLE'S HERALDIC TROMPE L'OEIL CARPET IN THE LOGGIA-LIKE ENTRANCE VESTIBULE.

OPPOSITE: A RUSTIC PAINT FINISH INSPIRED BY THE TILED FRIEZES OF THE PORTUGUESE VILLAS IN SINTRA.

AT HOME ON THE BEACH

Bali is a smallish island, ringed for the most part by white sand and palm-fringed shores. The earliest human inhabitants were at home on the beach some sixty thousand years ago, but with the exception of a few fishing villages, it was not until the age of Chinese trading vessels—at the time of Marco Polo, when the northern capital of Singaraja was an important entrepôt for the sandalwood trade—that coastal settlements started to spring up.

The oldest inscription in Bali is found on a stone pillar in Belanjong, South Sanur, on the southeast coast, dating back to the tenth century, the start of Java's and Bali's classic Hindu period. It is not surprising, then, that Sanur today is Bali's biggest and, one suspects, oldest surviving coastal community, with a large population of Brahmins and priests. Terraced, coral-walled sanctuaries from pre-Hindu times still dot the coast. The village architecture today is elegant and classical, with colonial influences from Denpasar's Urban Deco period; the village life is dynamic and full of ceremony.

It was in Sanur that Bali's first expatriates built beach houses in the 1930s, attracted as much by the patrician charms of the locals as by the balmy breezes and eastern seaboard. In 1950 Belgian painter Le Mayeur built an idyllic studio on Sanur Beach; the romantic garden was replete with bare-breasted, Junoesque gardeners—if we regard his art as an accurate record. It is now a much-visited museum. In the 1960s a young Jakartan film student, Wija Waworuntu, and his English wife, Judith, carved a sandy track through the palm groves south of Sindu village and built a few cottages on the beach. The complex was called Tanjung Sari (Cape of Flowers) and quickly became a legend that begot many imitators. For twenty years it was the place to stay, and it inspired hotel impresario Adrian Zecha to start his now celebrated Aman resorts. Australian artist Donald Friend came to Bali in 1967, arriving at the Tanjung Sari on the same day as English diplomat and seasoned Asia hand Chris Carlisle. Together with Wija Waworuntu they bought up land that is now the Batu Jimbar estates and the Bali Hyatt, Southeast Asia's first truly glamorous beachside grand hotel. They built a series of homes along the Batu Jimbar strip, all picturesque, all gaily Balinese. Sri Lankan master architect Geoffrey Bawa was introduced to the scene by Friend in 1973; he revamped Friend's now palatial spread, adding a museum for his collection of early bronzes and a number of other buildings. When Friend left the island under a cloud in 1984, the house was acquired by Adrian Zecha and ripped apart by architect du jour Ed Tuttle, whose Amanpuri Hotel on the Thai island of Phuket has long been the premier resort in Asia. Friend's garden, then one of Bali's finest, was scattered to the winds, and a rather imposing and polished house took the place of the crusty old maestro's harem. All these goings-on provided much fuel—of both the gossip and architectural varieties—for the fantasy furnace, as for twenty-five years the Donald Friend house had been regarded as the epitome of "at home on the beach" in Bali. It inspired an industry of dream homes and attracted the likes of Japanese tycoon Kajima (President Suharto, his golfing buddy, once slept in Kajima's house), couturier John Galliano, Yoko Ono, the Gstaad set led by the younger members of the Santo-Domingo clan, and a legion of *aman*-wannabes, film stars, rock stars, and even Fergie (Zecha's greatest coup).

Sanur is the place where the Dutch landed in colonial times and took South Bali in a shocking series of battles. It is also the site of Bali's first and only high-rise, the eleven-story Hotel Bali Beach (after this mistake it was forbidden to build higher than the coconut trees). Sanur was the launching pad for upmarket tourism in the 1970s: Batu Jimbar had Bali's first air-conditioned room (to cater to Judith Waworuntu's Fendi furs) and was a training ground for the Miller girls, the 1970s answer to Babe Paley and the rest of the Cushing sisters. It could be said that Sanur is Bali's Hyannis Port.

On the opposite coast, the sleepy Chinese trading post of Kuta underwent a transformation of a completely different kind. Unlike Sanur, its strait-bound competitor, Kuta faces the Indian Ocean and has been blessed with wide-open beaches and rolling surf. In the nineteenth century Danish trader Mads Lange established a base here and put Kuta on the international map. In earlier centuries, the destination of Portuguese sailors and Hindu pilgrim priests had been the Peti Tenget estuary to the north of the Kuta and Legian beaches, but by the 1970s only a tiny harbormaster's house, in the whitewashed coastal style, remained.

In the 1930s American writer Louis Koke wrote a book, *Our Hotel in Bali,* about building a house on Kuta Beach. Revolutionary rabble-rouser Ketut Tantri (former scriptwriter for the *Our Gang* movies and friend of Vicki "Grand Hotel" Baum, another Bali habitué) was a permanent fixture on Kuta Beach throughout the tumultuous 1940s and during the glory days of her friend President Sukarno in the 1950s, when she wrote her fantasy memoirs *Revolt in Paradise*. Both Koke's and Ketut Tantri's house complexes were basic and rustic, perched on the primary dunes facing the rolling waves and seductive sunsets. The Balinese lived inland in small village clusters away from the malign spirits that haunted the cemeteries by the sea; their livelihood relied more on rice cultivation than on fishing.

It was into this idyllic coastal scene with its coconut palm groves, bamboo huts, and grazing cows that the first hippies and the first surfies stepped in the mid-1960s. Soon Kuta was an established node on the Darwin-Ibiza backpackers' route; out of these humble beginnings, with one Chinese restaurant serving magic mushroom omelettes and one lean-to on the beach offering black rice pudding to spent surfers, grew a multiheaded Medusa of merchandising that now rivals Patonga, Pakpong, and Waikiki. The salad days of the 1930s became the fruit salad and muesli days of the 1960s. By the 1980s, hedonism had hardened. At that time I wrote a piece on the west coast tourist strip that still sums up the scene quite well:

There is something hypnotic about the west coast between 3 P.M. and 4 P.M.: the silhouettes of the perfectly formed hover, like sirens in suspended mirage. Lurex G-strings glitter like so many wing-jets against an azure sky. Balinese and Japanese surfies vie for the meanest neo-Waikiki scowls and Darwin accents. Tireless saleswomen and marauding masseurs ply their wares like bedouins in the Sahara of the satay-satiated. Upper Legian beachside is Bali's highway of hedonism.

Duck inland for a look at the local dream homes of the expatriates—pretty exotic. Stop first at "66" for perfectly prepared pizza and a gawk at the latest combination of sequined fez and jersey tank top—the perennial fashion of these dinosaurs of the counterculture. Just down the beach, in front of Blue Ocean and Sunset bungalows, is where the "real" people go. At any one time along this strip, you will see half the cast of the original London production of Hair!

From the very hip and international Blue Ocean belt, walk south through "Little Australia," the broad strip of bubbling bellies and dulcet-toned day-feeding marsupials that runs from the Kuta Palace Hotel to Pertamina Cottages, hard on the airport. Walk briskly to the Yasa Samudra Hotel, passing some world-class surfing by Kuta teenagers to the west. Wait for the sunset, when the busloads of domestic tourists in party dress descend on the beach, to wade ankle-deep in the Indian Ocean and ogle the tourists. Post-sunset, visit Made's Warung for happy hour and see the real people from Blue Ocean fully dressed.

Beach life in expatriate Bali thus has two sides on two different coasts: the solid citizens of Sanur versus the solidly soporific of Kuta-Legian; the morning glories in their vintage Mercedes versus the late-night lounge lizards in Versuses and Voyages.

The Kuta Balinese and the Sanur Balinese have moved back a block to allow for the onslaught of art shops and have, sadly, let their coastlines be ruined by uncontrolled development. It seems that the tourists have taken over: at home on the beach is now more about suntans and serial suppers than palm-fringed shores. Architecturally, an unprecedented expatriate building boom has given rise to some real exotics, in the Bali tradition—the Rice Barn Cellular and the Barlow Beyondo-Milano styles, to name just two. And to balance things up, Balinese surfers are now among the best in the world.

But the gamelan beat goes on. I still regularly find myself walking in a procession with thousands of Balinese in their processional best at dawn, turning past the hostile entrance to the Hard Rock Hotel onto a perfect beach aglow with golden morning light. The cows still graze amid the parked Yamahas, and the spirit of Janique, Miss Kuta of 1964, now Miss Asian Businesswoman of 1988, with her pan-Asian string of Poppies hotels, still serves black rice pudding under the beach heliotrope.

STATELY SEASIDE
SERENADE

THE WEST COAST BEACHES BETWEEN KUTA AND TANAH LOT have an eerie beauty; the afternoon light and dry beachside heat make for an atmosphere of heightened intensity.

Design- and project-managed by Bali-based Australian architect Ross Franklin for local studio UNIKON, Villa Atas Ombak exudes New World charm: it is a brash arriviste in the Saint-Tropez division of the "Balinasia" movement—a postmodern school that eschews Balinese decorative detail but keeps the bones of the Asian pavilion style intact. Immensely popular with supermodels and publicity-shy movie stars (who love the cracks and crevices of the west coast scene, Bali's answer to Ibiza), Bali's beachside mega-villa market is here to stay.

Clever interior design and fabulous natural vegetation in the simple gardens saves the compound from being just another beachside spread with a big pool. It also has a lovely sense of

ABOVE: A SERENE SIDE WATER GARDEN HUGS
A COVERED WALKWAY.

RIGHT: LIKE ALBINO STEALTH JETS OVER THE SUEZ CANAL,
BEACH UMBRELLAS GUARD A FRESHLY PALM-FRINGED SHORE.

52

seclusion: the property is protected by a lagoon to the north, a river to the east, and a broad expanse of Indian Ocean beach to the west. To the south is a similar estate, the former Garuda Park, belonging to Mark Shand, the brother of Camilla Parker Bowles, and Hon. Harry Fane (an exclusive place, where "friends of friends" were sent away).

The compound's beachfront was formerly the northern-most pandanus grove of the North Oberoi Beach Nookie Watch: from the inner recesses of the pandanus thickets a tire-less band of local voyeurs kept track of beachside trysts. Against the advice of the architect, the villa's owner chose to destroy this heritage habitat so that visiting rock stars could see the whole horizon and experience the full brunt of the westerly monsoon winds. The house sits proud and unadorned on its site, protect-ed from prying eyes by an unusually high hump of primary dune and a thick band of sea grape that has been replanted along the former pandanus belt. A single row of evenly spaced coconut

OPPOSITE: A STRIKING CANVAS BY SAYAN-BASED IAN VAN WIERINGEN LOOMS LARGE OVER A SIMPLE BED AND ATTENDANT TABLES. THE PRIM-ITIVE CHEST AT THE BED'S FOOT IS A NICE STORAGE BIN FROM CENTRAL SULAWESI.

ABOVE: THE PALATIAL POOL REFLECTS THE HANDSOME PAVILION ARCHITECTURE.

BELOW: A CHINESE ALTAR TABLE HAS ANOTHER LIFE AS A HALLWAY ACCENT PIECE.

ABOVE: ARCHITECT FRANKLIN
REPEATED THE STRONG DIAGONAL
LINES OF THE ROOF STRUCTURE
IN THE PATTERN ON THE SALON'S
TERRAZZO FLOOR.

trees keeps silent watch over a beachside pool: it would be a touch *triste* but for the austere majesty of the view west. The volcanoes of East Java beckon from the far horizon, and the deep blue of the Indian Ocean blends seamlessly with the pool and the big azure sky.

The house itself is simple, like a Roman villa; the words SPACIOUS and STYLISH spelled out in Roman capitals appear in the visitor's mind. The furniture and artwork selections are clever and unusual: small "bouquets" of primitive art litter base-board skirtings and tabletops. Water gardens and clever timber walkways are worked into the design at the cozier entrance area of the house, away from the beach, where a delightful tropical garden flourishes.

The look is minimal, the effect, grand—partly because of the great space, a luxury in Balinese real estate. (Most pretenders to the upper echelons are somewhat cramped.)

Monsoon sunsets and full-moon nights are incredible viewed from the chic confines of this *palazzo splendido;* had Tiberius known about Upper Legian, he might have eschewed Sperlonga.

LEFT: THE STAIRS ARE CLEAN AND SIMPLE: INLAID, POLISHED TERRAZZO.

BELOW: A DRUM FROM AN OLD LOMBOK MOSQUE; COLLECTIBLES FROM OTHER ETHNIC PARTS OF THE ARCHIPELAGO LINE THE SALON'S SKIRTINGS.

INDIAN OCEAN ESTATE

ROLF AND HELEN VON BUEREN ARE GREAT CREATORS: IN their thirty-five years together they have never paused in their passionate quest for beauty. In Bangkok they created a magical inner-city oasis—traditional Thai bungalows set in splendid canalside gardens—that is the envy of all Southeast Asia. An invitation to one of their "high Thai style" soirees (Thai and international guests always well balanced) is much sought after by the Bangkok-bound.

They produced the best-looking boys of their generation (with the best Thai manners and the most gorgeous jet-set girl-friends). The boys now work with Helen and Rolf in designing and producing *objets de vivre* (jewelry and exotic housewares) for their beautifully crafted chain of Lotus boutiques, found in only the most discerning hotels—the Raffles in Singapore, the Amanpuri in Phuket, and Brown's in London, among others.

When it came to doing their Bali retreat in 1979, they wanted only the best, naturally; in this case what was "best" for Bali.

ABOVE: THE OPEN-SIDED MEZZANINE BEDROOM HAS A
TENT-LIKE BED IN THE MIDDLE.

RIGHT: THE VIEW WEST, ACROSS THE LAGOON, TO THE
INDIAN OCEAN FROM THE VON BUERENS' TREEHOUSE.

The team split into two: Rolf looked for land, while Helen started training the cooks and planning their outfits. Soon they had reached first base: Rolf found a perfect island at Brawa, six acres surrounding a lagoon on an Indian Ocean beach well north of Legian. Helen decreed that all guests to their future compound must be more Balinese than the Balinese in what they eat, wear, and watch.

"Brawa Baywatch" was born!

Rolf had been to Bali many times since the 1960s, when he started his career as a businessman and art collector in Bangkok, and he knew he didn't want a "rich man's villa." His dream was to create a "collective" of like-minded friends, all bon vivants, all Bali-besotted, or soon to be, who would come together once a year and live the humble life—give or take a command gamelan performance or two—in a beautiful Balinese setting. No swimming pools, ostentatious interiors, or "foreign" architecture would be allowed. Peter Muller, the Balinese architecture expert, was asked to design the compound shortly after his success at the Bali Oberoi. He declined and flicked the job to this writer.

It was my first job as an architect: it had been offered, I felt, on the basis of my show home in Sanur—a tiny compound of

ultratraditional Balinese pavilions built in 1980–86. I met Rolf and was delighted by his enthusiasm, if awed by his Bavarian bravado, and signed up for eight years' work.

The brief was to create a utopian Balinese village using only traditional architecture—which was right up my alley. We first built a sunset pavilion on the dreamy lagoon to serve as a communal sitting room/"banquet hall." It had an outrider pavilion, with a Thai-style platform bed, right on the lagoon's edge. The pavilion's feature wall was designed by Nyoman Gunarsa, now

OPPOSITE, ABOVE, AND LEFT: THE AUTHOR'S FIRM MODELED THE ESTATE'S GARDENS ON THOSE OF THE OLD COLONIAL BUNGALOWS OF PENANG AND GOA, WITH BALINESE DECORATIVE ACCENTS— GATES, WALLS, AND PERGOLAS.

ABOVE AND OPPOSITE: THE PROPERTY'S WESTERN BOUND-
ARY SURVEYS THE RICE FIELDS OF NEARBY BRAWA VILLAGE—
A VIEW THAT STRETCHES TO GLORIOUS MOUNT AGUNG,
BALI'S ANSWER TO MOUNT FUJI.

one of Bali's most sought-after artists.

Next came Rolf and Helen's compound. They chose a plot
with stunning views to the rice fields that rolled down to the back
of the estate (the "island" was in fact a delta promontory, confined
by two rivers that fed the lagoon). I designed four pavilions, using
pavilion pieces procured by Rolf's loyal henchman Max Weber, a
chef at the Hotel Bali Beach (now the Grand Bali Beach) who
shared Rolf's passion both for the architecture of East Bali and for
bargains. No expense was spared in time and energy, however, in
finding the rarest cloths to make the futons and floor cushions
(house rules eschewed Western furniture) and in fashioning the
most artistic quasi-traditional ice buckets, egg cups, and stationery.
It was Robinson Crusoe meets the last flutter of the Weimar
Republic! I built three Balinese gates for this compound, a lotus
lake, and a bamboo bridge; the final result was enchanting.

The next project on the site was a duplex villa for charming
Bavarian industrialist Dr. Jorge Otto Wiegand, who wanted a
slightly less authentic holiday home. I created a hybrid Bale

(pavilion) Agung duplex with an open-sided master suite on the
first floor and an elaborate garden bathroom below: a seductive
view from the main living terrace looked down the mouth of a
river estuary and then across the lagoon to an expanse of the
Indian Ocean. Yet another "deluxe" Bali gate and another lotus
lake set in more conventional tropical villa gardens completed
the picture.

Various new complexes were added over the next decade of
building. More land was acquired adjacent to the estate, more
folly gates were fashioned, and summer after summer of party-
planning stretched to eternity—each year even more dancing
girls were added for an ever-expanding guest list.

Nineteen ninety-eight was a bumper year for the compound: it celebrated its twentieth anniversary (no mean feat
considering the fickle nature of Balinese real estate develop-
ments). The touristic sprawl, which Rolf always disdained, had
stopped well short of the compound's southern border; the
lagoon had survived attempts by corrupt developers to fill it in;
and Rolf and Helen still looked young and vital after the birth
of their first grandchild.

A huge five-day party was held to celebrate the marriage of
Rolf and Helen's eldest son, Sri, to Rai, a Hong Kong debutante.
Le tout Bangkok and a representative slice of the upper crusts of
London, Munich, Hong Kong, and Jakarta descended on the
compound in regal Balinese and Thai attire. The lagoon was lit
with one thousand floating candles, the gates to all compounds
flung open, and the gardens "stacked" with bouquets of sweet-
smelling tuberoses for a series of *soirees de gala*. H.R.H. Aisyha,
the maharani of Jaipur, was guest of honor, presiding regally
over the biggest and brightest garden party Bali has ever seen.

After the ball was over, the Von Buerens stayed on for
another two weeks to savor the recently revamped grounds.

The passage of time has been kind: none of the thirty-odd
buildings are visible from the beach, and Mount Agung *is* still
visible from the Von Buerens' veranda. Rolf and Helen, their
ever-extending family, and their court and compound are a rare
exception to the rule on the west coast. Long may they reign!

AT HOME IN THE RICE FIELDS

FROM THE AIR BALI APPEARS covered with beautifully are often called the most ALMOST COMPLETELY sculpted rice terraces. They beautiful in the world; indeed, the Balinese take great pride in every detail of their agricultural cycle. There are temples to Dewi Sri, the rice goddess, in every village: some areas even have a shrine in the propitious northeast corner of every field. There are massive annual rat cremations to ward off insect plagues; ten-day festivals on the crater lakes, at which the island's farmers offer animal sacrifices to Dewi Danau, the goddess of the crater lakes; and ancient organizations, called *subak,* that control the partitioning of irrigation canals, both large and small. One of the prettiest sights in Bali is the teams of villagers in multihued shirts beating and husking grain, as battalions of ducks scramble for the discarded husks. Against the backdrop of golden harvest fields, the farmers' shirts wave like regatta flags.

Although few Balinese actually live in the rice fields, some farmers build *pondok* huts in which they might store equipment, cook a lunchtime meal, or take a siesta. In some areas these pondoks are quite elaborate, like weekend shacks, and can be souped up to include livestock pens, duck ponds, and spice gardens.

In 1970 Australian poet John Darling rented some land from the family of the illustrious artist Gusti Nyoman Lempad and built Bali's first designer pondok, complete with packed-mud floors, woven bamboo screen walls, and radio antennae for his daily intake of cricket via the BBC. He had a cow and a vegetable patch and used only building methods found in the pondok styles of the island. All the compound's bamboo pavilions had windows opening out onto the rice fields. In fact the only approach to the house was via the small paths, called *pundukan,* that run along the sides of the paddies. He bathed in the spring coursing through the ravine below and took his morning coffee gazing across the valley at the glistening cone of Mount Agung.

In 1975 local designer Putu Suarsa, from the traditional village of Sidakarya in the island's southern "bread basket" (rice bin?), built a series of bungalows in the rice fields. He called the complex Pondok Bamboo, as the majority of the buildings and the furniture were constructed of bamboo. It was here that the island's first big bamboo sofa was crafted, based on a design by Australian Terry Stanton. Suarsa's pondok hit the cover of *The World of Interiors* magazine in the U.K., and an era of interest in this sort of ethnic chic was ushered in. Suarsa's only concessions to the rental market were terra-cotta floors, lovingly polished using the desiccated-coconut method, and baked brick walls in the bedroom sections, to keep out the coastal crabs.

Since these early pioneers, foreigners who prefer the gentle rhythm of a rural community lifestyle have chosen rice-field sites, with their enchanting cavalcade of agricultural activity, over the beach scene or the panoramas of the ridges. At the same time, many young Balinese are deserting the rural life for jobs in hotels on the coast.

Hotel developers are also cashing in on the seductive panoramas—the Amandari, the Hotel Saba Bay, and the Bali Nirwana all enjoy prime rice-field views. Such properties are developed under the quaint banner "agritourism."

Old pondok buildings are fast disappearing from the rice fields as cooperative rice farming takes over from family plots and more permanent huts are built to replace the charming cottages.

In the rice fields near the Seminyak-Kerobokan area of Kuta, expatriate dream homes, variously styled after Balinese rice lofts or bingo palaces, are popping up like wildflowers. This construction has tended to pollute the environment and dilute the agricultural lifestyle. As a result, rice fields have become suburbs for "Lanai lovelies"—those loyal devotees of Legian-Kuta's café society, the direct descendants of the first hippies who hopped off the trail before Goa or Penang. Where once buffalo roamed, dinosaurs of the counterculture now pick their way along narrow lanes.

In the 1990s some seriously chic homesteads started to appear in rice-growing areas: Linda Garland's ravishing estate and John and Cynthia Hardy's "official residence," Long Bang, both made *Architectural Digest.* Indeed, the ultimate glossy has devoted an article a month to Balinese or Javanese houses during this period, and the attention is fully justified, for it has been a fertile time for design.

The entry of my own office, P. T. Wijaya, was the Puri Canggu Mertha; this was one of many villa complexes built in the rice fields near the fishing village and surfer's paradise of Canggu, near Kuta. It was designed to attract the attention of vacationers from Jakarta, Singapore, and Sydney who wanted to be near the fleshpots yet in the rice fields. Like John Darling's pondok retreat, the complex faces the river and the bamboo groves beyond but opens out on its sides to deep views of the fairyland silhouettes of distant temples across the rice fields.

At home in the rice fields the clip-clop of the water buffalos that plow the flooded paddies and the sirenlike hum of the tall wind flutes, erected by farmers to please the rice goddess, accompany the lazy days of Hindu holidaymakers.

HEALER'S HACIENDA
IN RURAL SPLENDOR

MELBOURNE FORD DEALER CAM DAWSON CAME TO BALI IN 1974 for a quiet holiday. During the stay, however, his life changed dramatically. His son Tony, aged ten, had a vision, his first, in the "palace" of Cam's driver, the good prince Agung Kaleran of Peliatan, near Ubud. It was quickly divined that young Tony was an incarnation of the prince's uncle, who had died a decade previously, and the Dawson family was thus adopted by the Peliatan palace (famous for first sending Legong dancers to Versailles in 1938) and nurtured as a cross-cultural catch.

Now, it must here be said that many an incarnation has been invented by the wily Balinese in the name of real estate, but the Peliatan princes are men of learning, and the Dawson clan was a rare catch indeed: they were to grow, over the next decade, into chiropractics' answer to the singing Von Trapps!

In 1979 Cam, with the help of his Peliatan "family," acquired a small house with land in the rice fields, built by artist Hans Snel

ABOVE AND RIGHT: ECLECTIC INTERIOR PIECES, CULLED FROM THE ARTSHOPS THAT LINE THE ROAD FROM THE AIRPORT TO UBUD, ARE DE RIGUEUR IN THE HOMES OF THE HILL TRIBES.

for a UN doctor on the outskirts of Sayan village. The land was on the less glamorous eastern side of the village, far south of Sayan's notorious "Lovers' Leap" (the artist's ridge where high rollers like Margaret Mead had hung out).

The Dawsons built a simple L-shaped cottage with wide verandas for improptu healing treatments. The affable Cam was happy on the wrong side of the tracks in the rice fields with his family of embryonic wizards and his few, loyal Balinese friends. One such friend was Pak Gading, a masseur-healer from behind the Peliatan palace who taught the crusty Aussie a few tricks of the Balinese healer's trade. Cam returned to Australia and studied chiropractic healing, eventually deserting the rows of Fords' best for rows of bent brunettes.

Returning to Sayan in 1981, Cam quickly developed a reputation among the Balinese as a miracle healer: farmers were soon calling on "Tuan Doctor" with their aches and pains.

From 1990 to 1998 the house fell into disrepair. Cam and his sons were building up a successful healing center in Geelong, near Melbourne, and had little time for their exotic Balinese life.

In 1998 Sydney decorator Arthur Karvan of Karvan and Little (formerly Arthur's of Kandos) was brought in to work on the property, and waved wand after wand of decorative enchantment. The humble rice-paddy-side abode was soon unrecognizable: tension-edge water features came as celadon plunge pools and pixie-glen duck ponds; "Meet Me in St. Louis" stripes fluttered like eyelids over built-in commodes and tasteful trompe l'oeil. A "double-header" massage pavilion was added with mismatched madras-stripe canvas blinds and in it Ketut and Siti, the rakish Balinese master couple of deep tissue therapy, kneaded away the woes of waves of wanderers.

The decorator's touch *has* made the compound look "lived in," as the saying goes, "but by somebody else." Cam and Tony, though, still reign supreme in this cosmopolitan retreat—the boundary wall to the rice fields remains low, and the passing parade of rice farmers continue to offer smiles a mile wide.

Cam still receives patients (this writer one of them) on his frequent visits to his beloved isle. His method has become more

OPPOSITE: THE MAIN HOUSE VIEWED FROM THE GREEN SLATE-TILED SWIMMING POOL.

RIGHT: SAMSAN DESIGN'S PLAYFUL TRACERY AROUND THE DOOR FRAME OF AN "ACCENT DOOR" FROM NEARBY LOMBOK ISLAND.

mystical, in a nice Balinese way: gongs and Hindu soothsaying are used more and more in combination with video (Cam is handy with his Sony) and son Tony's less karmic adjustments. The rice-field scene still drifts up to the foot of every massage bed.

Decorator Karvan is a recent convert to Tibetan Buddhism, after years as a club owner in Sydney's notorious King's Cross, and guests are received in the "White Lotus Inn" at the reception pavilion—a charming colonial terrace looking east over the golden paddy fields. Arrivees generally get a warm handshake and a grim prognosis from Cam before being swept up by the house's staff.

There's a distinct feeling of the gentleman's haunt about the spruced-up verandas, and more marble bench tops than you can point a bone at. A healthy sprinkling of garden artifacts from the Wijaya Classics Range has enhanced the outdoor courtyard areas—and this being Sayan village (famous for its arty ethnic cottages), the plants are lovingly maintained within the existing grove of frangipani (or plumeria) amid statues plied with offerings.

Interior finishes are a homage to Stephen Little's Bali work, and the choice of furniture is quaintly colonial with clever use of distressed finishes (Arthur's specialty). Cam and Tony are often around to click your chakras into shape if the onslaught of gorgeousness gets too tense-making.

HIGH COZY IN THE HIGH COUNTRY

THE 1990S SAW A REAL ESTATE EXPLOSION IN BALI'S KUTA-Kerobokan counties—a cottage industry in cottages, you might say. Various style books inspired multifarious dream-home hybrids—summer love nests and winter rental properties. The sense of an oasis of calm to be had in many of these "hand-woven" wonders is a part of their charm. One of the prettiest of these is Jane Corser's aptly named Villa Bella off the main Kuta-Denpasar mall and around the back of a long mile of art shops.

In the Villa Bella one steps through the tight gate to glimpse, through undulating "terraces" of architecture, the delightful pastoral view of rice fields and bamboo groves. This would be tight and trite, considering the limited space, but for the "giving" nature of the architectural treatments (all soft corners and sun-soaked colors) and the clever roll of the miniature parkland garden.

ABOVE: ONE OF THE MANY PICTURESQUE
AXIAL VIEWS IN THE COTTAGE.

LEFT: THE RICE FIELDS LAP LIKE WAVES ONTO
A HAMMOCK-STRUNG POOL TERRACE.

75

OPPOSITE, RIGHT, AND BELOW: ELEMENTS FROM JAVANESE TRADITIONAL HOUSES HAVE BEEN USED AMONG THE MORE MOROCCAN MOLDED CONCRETE ARCHITECTURE. AT RIGHT, A TRADITIONAL JAVANESE REGENCY SETTEE IS PARKED, FACING THE VIEW, AMONG BASKETS OF TUBEROSES, THE ULTIMATE EXPATRIATE ACCESSORY.

Jane Corser, the house's owner and designer, is a lover of gardens and a clever decorator—what the house lacks in architectural sophistication is more than compensated for in deft decorative touches. These are culled from many lands—India, Greece, and Mexico, not to mention the Indonesian islands of

Java, Bali, and Madura. In fact, in the house's interiors Corser has captured a spirit to refresh the weary world traveler—everything is easy and carefree.

Terraces appear as banquettes of molded cement; clothes are kept on ornamental wrought-iron racks; there are niches with color-coordinated *objets trouvés* rather than the usual clutter, found in many coastal cottages, of carved items nailed to the wall. The garden views, glimpsed through cleverly sculpted terraces, and the occasional distressed-finish armoire are the real artworks, apart from the odd Frida Kahlo portrait (Frida is the patron saint of the Legian rag trade, it would seem).

Sitting in the opera-box-like terraces off either bedroom, surveying the delightfully framed views to the golden rice terraces across the stream, one is transported back in time to the 1980s, when buffalo roamed the lanes of Legian rather than crack dealers. Back to the salad days of free love and Frisbees and pineapple lassi.

Oh, the bliss!

Bliss-making is the Villa.

Brava la Bella.

LEFT: A GIANT BEADED POUF WITH
ATTENDANT MOSQUITO-NET-DRAPED
COLONIAL BED—THE "WEEPING BRIDE"
OF AN ANNIE HALL-ESQUE BALI.

ABOVE: THESE FAUX WINDOWS, INVENT-
ED BY CAROLE MULLER FOR A "COST
PLUS" CATALOG IN 1983, ARE A FIRM
FAVORITE ACROSS THE EQUATOR.
WIDELY KNOWN AS "PRISON WINDOWS"
IN SINGAPORE, THEY LIVEN UP AN
ARCHITECTURAL CUL DE SAC WITH THEIR
PERSPECTIVE-ENHANCING PROPERTIES.

BELOW AND OPPOSITE: A MARQUIS DE
SADE TOUCH, IN COLORED TERRAZZO,
BRINGS DRAMA TO THIS WALLED
BATHROOM COURT.

RICE FIELD CHIC

The Dutch have a word, *GEZELLIG*, for a decorative style that is happy and nurturing. It is designer Hinke Zieck's favorite word and the driving force behind her talent. Old Indonesia hands, she and her husband Walter Zieck moved to their present house in the rice fields south of Sidakarya village after a stint in the suburbs of nearby Sanur. The pondok-style house is one of five in a compound called Big Bamboo and owned by local impresario Putu Suarsa. Putu's own house, in the same compound of pondoks, was the first Balinese house to grace the pages of *The World of Interiors,* in 1989. His bamboo architecture artistry is a noble partner for Hinke's international velvet and distressed-finishing-school look.

The Ziecks' house is compact; a tiny pebbled court with one gnarled frangipani placed off-center announces the front door. The garden spaces therefore function as outdoor living areas full of Hinke's own garden furniture and artifacts. Inside, rooms are full, and full of surprises—everything is embroidered or trimmed with fresh exuberant color, even Walter's dashing silver

LEFT AND ABOVE: Suarsa's imaginative use
of bamboo and Hinke's lively use of
color are perfect playmates.

81

ponytail. Frequent trips to Morocco have borne exotic fruits: touches from North Africa do not look out of place in the cleverly crafted interiors.

Hinke's own paintings are everywhere—on easels, leaning against walls, competing for surface space with piles of art books and original flower arrangements. Three maids, three dogs, and Walter's office corner also find room amid Hinke's artistic largesse. This Technicolor whirlwind of a woman is herself a work of art: always immaculately groomed, in the tradition of the great decorators. Her fashion sense also signals her flair for the free-floating and the original. Her dinner parties are fun, al fresco affairs with delicious Italian food (Positano is the Ziecks' "heaven on earth") and Dutch Colonial desserts. From Hinke's success at home, on show, in the rice fields, she has garnered many prestigious commissions—the spa at the Four Seasons

LEFT AND ABOVE: A poly-
chrome Madurese bed
anchors the loggialike
living room.

OPPOSITE: Prodigious painter
Hinke is always halfway
through one canvas or
another. This poignant portrait is a perfect complement
for the Javanese armoire in
the room's corner.

LEFT: COLONIAL PIECES SIT
WELL WITH THE CLASSICAL
BALINESE ARCHITECTURE.

RIGHT AND BELOW: HINKE
HAS FILLED HER BALI HOME
WITH THE CURVACEOUS AND
THE COLORFUL.

Resort, Jimbaran, a complete revamp of the Four Seasons
Resort, Maldives, and other private commissions.

Hinke's bright Arts and Crafts style is a fresh addition to
the design scene, and one hopes she will continue to liven up
the ultra-safe interiors of the island's hotels.

OPPOSITE: THE HARD BLACK METALWORK OF
A CANDELABRA AND GARDEN CHAIRS FROM
HINKE'S ATELIER CONTRAST STARKLY WITH
SUARSA'S BALI BRICK DETAILING AND FAUX
ADOBE PLASTERING.

AT HOME IN THE RICE FIELDS

BRAZILIAN BARONIAL

THIS HOUSE IN ISEH HAS HAD AN ILLUSTRIOUS PAST: painters Walter Spies and Theo Meyer did some of their best work in the mesmerizing mountain beauty that surrounds it. The house was originally a studio retreat built by legendary German artist Spies. In the 1950s, it became the base camp for writer Vicki Baum and the inspiration for her book *Night of the Purnama.* Swiss painter Theo Meyer restored the house after the devastation of the 1965 volcano. Also during the 1960s Meyer and his Balinese wife befriended the young prince of the neighboring village of Sidhemen—a dashing young nobleman with a brooding curiosity and expansive nature. The prince would woo waves of paradise seekers over the ensuing thirty-five years.

In 1985 Florentine writer Idanna Pucci, niece of the couturier Emilio Pucci, embarked on a makeover of the house, enlisting this writer in his capacity as aesthetic adviser to the terminally thrifty. The result was successful—the Pucci family is known for its excellent taste—but the noble houses of Sidhemen and Pucci were frequently at odds.

RIGHT: THE BREATHTAKING "UNDER THE VOLCANO" VIEW OF MAJESTIC MOUNT AGUNG FROM THE HOUSE'S TERRACE (ABOVE).

OPPOSITE: Bird's-nest ferns and Bismarckia palm fronds frame this picture postcard view of the guest pavilion, painted in the house colors, pink and pale green.

BELOW: From the room that was once the artist's studio, one steps up through an ornate East Balinese door to an intimate dining nook (right).

ABOVE, LEFT, AND RIGHT:
The house was worked on
during the interregnum
between the Pucci and the
Jesseriati occupancies by artist
Stephen Little, founder of
Samsara Designs. Everywhere,
in the window frames and wall
treatments, his light,
romantic touch can be felt.

In 1996 the lease passed to gentleman aesthete Hugo Jesseriati, a Brazilian with houses in Lisbon, New York, and Sanur. Hugo's love affair with Bali had begun during the fruit salad days of Bali-besottedness, when the "Kuta valkyrie," Princess Diane Von Furstenburg, "put a poem in a perfume" (as the packaging read) and the Miller girls roamed Batu Jimbar without titles or bodyguards.

By the mid-1990s Hugo, the master of Bali chic—who had up to this time entertained from various rental properties on the coast—needed a hacienda in which to receive his well-heeled guests. The house in Iseh fitted the bill. Here H.R.H. the maharani of Jaipur, national heroine Megawati Sukarnoputri, and the fabulously wealthy Isabella Goldsmith recently crossed the threshold on separate trajectories within five minutes of each other!

Today the exterior of the cottages is little changed from my Pucci renovation, but Hugo has, with the help of paint wizard Stephen Little, breathed life into the once austere interiors of the three-bedroom complex. Part Portuguese colonial, part

ABOVE AND RIGHT: THE MASTER BEDROOM CONTAINS SOME OF KEEN ANTIQUES HUNTER JESSERIATI'S TROVE OF ETHNIC ODDITIES, AND GOOD JAVANESE FURNITURE.

Balinese fantasy, the lovingly realized interiors are quite simply the prettiest set of rooms on the island. The neighboring prince still influences the life of the house: the culinary delights served here were invented to the exacting standards of East Balinese cuisine by Jesseriati and the chef trained in Sidhemen palace.

An invitation to spend a weekend in this house, with its drop-dead view of the volcano, its delicate, happy interiors, and its delightfully sophisticated host, is the hottest ticket among sophisticates in search of Shangri-la.

AN HEIRESS UPTOWN
IN THE RICE PADDIES

NEW AGE SOCIALITE ANGIE VESTEY HAS BEEN A BRIGHT star on the horizon since first coming to Bali in the 1980s. Heiress, good looker, bon vivant, and bright young thing, she lit up Legian like a Roman candle. She was destined to have the most glamorous house on the strip; here *Hello!* and other glossy magazines photograph really big stars of stage and screen.

As her architect she chose Ross Franklin, Legian's best, who was thrilled to be commissioned to design a dream home on a dream site—1.25 acres in the gorgeous rice fields near the surfing beach of Canggu. This was to be Bali's first Hollywood home—with British class. Franklin stuck to his well-honed repertoire of trad-mod Balinese architecture, realized by his trusty local lieutenant-builder Nyoman Gatra. The "estate" is shielded from the village of Semer's main lane by a high garden wall and large Balinese house gate, done in palace style. (In fact the name of the house is "Istana Semer," which translates as

LEFT: ARCHITECT ROSS FRANKLIN HAD A GRAND VISION FOR A FORMAL HOLLYWOOD-STYLE POOL IN THE DRAMATIC LANDSCAPE.

ABOVE: THE COVERED WALKWAY WITH ITS ENTICING AXIAL VISTA.

Semer Palace, a facetious allusion to what one visiting grandee describes as the "diabolical potholed track" to the property that existed at the time of the house's construction.) A covered walkway lined with handsome Javanese carved timber columns leads past juicy entrance courtyard gardens to the Javanese (*joglo* style) front door. For this special client, Franklin invented an Adams-style circular reception room for the house's heart. It is perched on a high point of the land so as to survey the stunning rice-field vistas. Off the main reception room are various wings—for servants, children, guests, and the master suite. Each of these wings is a separate Balinese thatched-roof bungalow, reached through interestingly decorated vestibule-links.

"Miss Vestey was very hands-on during all stages of the project," offers Franklin. "She was particularly involved in the choice of all architectural finishes"—such as the striking powdered limestone and cement floors and the decorative paint finishes by artist Stephen Little. Vestey did all the interior design herself: it is a jolly, practical mix of California style and colonial splendor. Two giant bamboo sofas, designed by Linda Garland, anchor the main room. All the rooms have ceilings that expose the beautiful craftmanship of the intricately thatched roofs. Together Vestey and Franklin chose the carved windows and Javanese housefronts that are a recurring decorative theme throughout the building. Little's muted trompe l'oeils provide the only splashes of color in most of the rooms.

OPPOSITE: BALI-BASED AUSTRALIAN ARTIST SHANE SWEENEY CREATED A BAS-RELIEF WALL BASED ON BOROBUDUR-ERA MYTHOLOGY FOR THE GALLERY THAT LEADS TO THE SUNKEN BATH.

LEFT: TROPICAL ELEMENTS IN A CORNER OF THE BATHROOM.

ABOVE: FROM VESTEY'S BEDROOM BALCONY ARE SEEN SOME OF THE PRETTIEST RICE FIELDS IN BALI.

Outside the color is provided by the lush gardens designed by Wayan "Braggie" Latra of Sidakarya village. Latra is one of Bali's best exponents of the naturalist Sanur school, which he helped found in 1979; he has worked at the Batu Jimbar and Bali Hyatt gardens. He cleverly wove some Balinese decorative touches into the quiet of the existing palm grove.

The house is famous for its sunset parties: *le tout Legian* and a lot of Saint-Tropez gather in the elegant reception room or on the poolside terrace to witness the brilliant sunset through the palms and across the rice fields. Framed by generous eaves and exotically carved windows, it is a vision worthy of all the work that went into this most glamorous of rice-field homes.

AT HOME IN THE GARDEN

BALI IS OFTEN DUBBED THE nesian officialdom. The Island of the Gods. In fact homes on Bali, and every temple has a superb garden, resplendent with shrines, striking artistic accents, and ornamental Oriental trees and shrubs such as frangipani and hibiscus.

GARDEN ISLAND BY INDO-Balinese themselves call it there are more temples than

It used to be that arrival in Bali meant that one's olfactory nerves were assailed by the pungent aroma of a billion incense sticks and floral offerings as the plane doors creaked open. Airport ramps and car exhaust have put an end to that, but the art of gardening still flourishes in Bali.

The traditional Balinese village house is a series of smallish pavilions set around a garden planted with freestanding flowering shrubs and shaded by fruit trees, such as guava or grapefruit. Even the palaces of Bali are not big edifices; but they do have elaborate gardens, large garden courtyards, and often moats around the royal house temples.

All Balinese love gardens because their culture is so entwined with their respect for nature. Flowers are used in headdresses and daily offerings, and are put behind the ears after prayers. The ornamental plumeria tree, called frangipani in the southern hemisphere, is very much the mascot of all Balinese temples, as its scented yellow-and-white flowers are the gods' favorite. The tree's shape also complements the rococo lines and flourishes of Balinese temple architecture.

In yesteryear the regents of Bali's nine regencies would build pleasure gardens in which to meditate and exercise their landscape designer skills.

The artist village of Ubud was particularly famous for its dewy gardens decorated with mossy statuary and water features. Water gardens were a staple of Balinese gardens because the lotus and the water lily, or *padma,* are the thrones of the gods in Hindu theology. High priests use water-lily petals to fashion the spirit effigies that accompany the soul on its elaborate ceremonial journey to reincarnation.

In 1906 the island's first ethnographer, Dutch artist Niewenkamp, recorded Bali's garden charms in lovingly executed, highly detailed drawings and etchings.

The Dutch colonial administration reached Bali only during the last 50 years of its 350-year tenure in the Indonesian archipelago, so the island was spared the petit bourgeois excesses that had spoiled the ancient garden traditions of Java and Sumatra until, remarkably, the final years of Suharto's New Order regime. Then herbaceous borders and Bambi statues spread like a skin rash across the archipelago, including, sadly, most of Bali's main roads. Gone are the stark Zen garden–like streetscapes of rows of mud-brick gates that used to enchant the visitor; but turn into any village home or hotel and you will be greeted by a leaf-perfect oasis.

The Sanur house garden is epitomized by white sandy paths and bougainvilleas; mountain house gardens, by stately tree ferns and shocking pink cordylines; the homes of the expatriates, by swimming pools demonstrating the latest trends in the hyperactive hotel-design community.

Australian architect Peter Muller's Bali Oberoi and Amandari hotels lent the island two pool types—the formal water-palace look in the former and the celadon green infinity-edge look in the latter—which have been much copied. Judith Waworuntu Tumbelaka Bell's first garden at the Tanjung Sari was a gem of coastal coziness, shaped in the English country-garden tradition of winding paths and picturesque pavilions.

Artists Jimmy Pandy and Donald Friend each turned their beachside palaces into museums of garden gorgeousness that utilized temple gates, water spouts, and spooky statuary in the High Balinese tradition. My work at the Bali Hyatt, the Bali Oberoi in Kuta, and the Amandari in Ubud during the years 1980 to 1990 proved a training ground for traditions now called Tropical Cotswolds and tropical planting schemes now erroneously called Balinese. These gardens were worked on by hundreds of clever artisans and are packed full of tricks picked up from both English gardens and the work of past masters on the island, including Donald Friend, John Darling, and Putu Suarsa. In 1991 the Four Seasons Resort in Jimbaran was completed and received much publicity for its Balinese village–like architecture and lavish Balinese-style gardens. The name Bali was now associated with garden hotels and dream hotels without rival in the tropical world. The island has supplanted Hawaii as the design capital of tropical garden art, with many of the masterworks done by Hawaiian landscape designers.

Books on Balinese flowers and gardening have flooded the market as the Balinese garden became to the 1990s homeowner in Southeast Asia what the Japanese garden had been to the Californian in the 1960s.

Houses are now built with the garden as the central theme; the Balinese have traditionally done their entertaining under shade structures in the garden, and the foreigners have followed suit. The "poodle in the puddle," "the moated marvel," and "the gnome-homes of the demi-indigenous" were satirical terms coined in the 1980s for the houses of converts who wanted to be at home in the garden.

GARDEN ARTIST'S
STUDIO HOME

THE VILLA BEBEK IN SANUR'S QUIET MERTASARI AREA WAS built in 1990 as the Bali residence of a very lovely lady, a former Miss Palm Beach (Sydney). It was my biggest private house commission as a designer and coincided with two other important jobs: a house garden for singer David Bowie on the island of Mustique, and the design of the Hotel Saba Bay on the coast of Central Bali, for which my office was not only architect but also interior designer and landscape designer. It was a very busy period indeed for our fledgling office, and the old adage, "If you want something done, give it to a busy person," proved true: all three jobs were finished pretty much on time and on budget. And the Villa Bebek benefited from getting the best pick of the crop in terms of antique doors and furniture.

As the Villa Bebek was also an investment for me (the client agreed to put two extra rental villas on the land) plus a great

ABOVE: POOLSIDE PERGOLA—THE BREAKFAST SPOT.

LEFT: THE TWO TWIN VILLAS OF VILLA BEBEK IN THE COLORFUL COMPOUND AS SEEN FROM THE BEDROOM OF THE THIRD VILLA.

opportunity for our office to do something grand on a smart residential street, the design team did their best to ensure a result to be proud of.

The architectural inspiration for the complex of three villas and a cottage was 1950s Balinese palace architecture—a blend of colonial and traditional styles. It also gives a nod to the Ceylonese details developed by Australian artist Donald Friend and architect Geoffrey Bawa in houses in Batu Jimbar (Sanur) during the 1960s. Linda Garland and Amir Rabik's 500-square-foot open pavilion in their Ubud home of the late 1980s was another great inspiration: I copied this vast open pavilion and placed it on top of a tower base as a giant living room-tree house.

The ten buildings were intricately interlocked through a network of gates and courtyards and garden walls. Ponds assisted in providing privacy (or at least assisted as barriers to keep the adjoining villas' dogs out!)

In 1997 I pulled down the walls separating the three villas of the property and redesigned the gardens. Villa Bebek entered a new phase as a multipurpose, multi-courtyard studio-house: my client's dream house was at last mine, all mine. Hyphens are often used to describe the Villa Bebek—office-showroom, traditional-modern, Bondi-Benares—like most New Balinese traditional homes of the 1990s. I use "New Balinese" to describe a

ABOVE: AN UNUSUAL MADURESE DRESSING TABLE IN THE TOWER BEDROOM.

NEAR RIGHT: A WOODEN STATUE OF THE GOD WISUU, PATRON SAINT OF GARDENERS, ON HIS BEAST OF BURDEN— THE EAGLE GARUDA—HANGING ON AN EAVE ADJACENT TO THE ENTRANCE.

FAR RIGHT: A SHRINE TO SARASWATI, GODDESS OF THE ARTS AND LITERATURE, GUARDS THE ENTRANCE TO THE SECRETARY'S ROOM.

OPPOSITE: THE AUTHOR'S OFFICE: SUMATRAN LONGHOUSE "LIONS" FLANK THE ENTRANCE TO AN INTERIOR BATHED IN LIGHT.

LEFT: A LEAN-TO ROOF OFF THE
ARCHITECT'S STUDIO SERVES AS
A BREAKOUT ZONE.

BELOW: THE MOROCCAN-
THEMED BLUE ROOM, WHICH
WAS ADDED AFTER THE
AUTHOR'S VISIT TO
MARRAKESH.

OPPOSITE: IN THE SITTING
ROOM ARE CUSHIONS FROM
CASABLANCA, A MIRROR
DESIGNED BY ED TUTTLE
FOR THE BALLROOM OF THE
HOTEL BOROBUDUR IN
JAKARTA, AND A LOUNGE CHAIR
DESIGNED BY JAKARTA-BASED
ARCHITECT JAYA IBRAHIM.

RIGHT: A SOAPSTONE CARVING
FROM A VILLAGE OUTSIDE
MARRAKESH SITS IN A GARDEN
WALL NICHE.

OPPOSITE: ONE OF MANY VISTAS ACROSS POND, COURTYARD, AND PERGOLA.

ABOVE: A CARVED BALINESE WINDOW PAINTED BY STEPHEN LITTLE.

RIGHT: THE CENTRAL COURTYARD, FROM THE AUTHOR'S DESK.

trend, in the expatriate building boom, for quasi-traditional homes for the quasi-Balinese. More than any other island paradise, Bali captures the imagination of her visitors, and Bali's New Age novices generally become amateur architects with princely passions. I put myself in this category, but I am perhaps more experienced than most, having spent fifteen years living as a feudal upstart in mini-palaces across the island.

The Villa Bebek's temple and gates, indeed the layout of the whole compound and the style of the gardens, is classically Balinese in a way that few Balinese mini-palaces still are. The compound has twelve pavilions and thirty-six courtyard gardens: each tropical pavilion opens onto garden terraces on at least two sides. These terraces link through a labyrinth of paths, ponds, pergolas, and internal Balinese gateways to rooms stacked with either antiques or drawing boards. The houses' interiors are annuals, not perennials—major changes are wrought overnight to accommodate the expectations of guests

or to provide a new studio for a project in progress. It has been said that Balinese traditional architecture is like a big box of Lego blocks, so adaptable is it to modification and change. Tropical gardens too are fun to rearrange—the Villa Bebek gardens have monthly overhauls as a new light or planter arrives for a test run. The name of the compound implies a sense of irreverence that continues through the interior design: Matador lamps guard "decommissioned" Chinese altar tables; Stephen Little's OSRAM light-box fridge (a dadaist marvel) finds a home in the ornate Marrakeshi suite; a beyond-kitsch T-shirt showing Diana, the Princess of Wales (a courtyard favorite) is draped at the feet of three ancestor figures from Borneo. The compound is not trying to be outrageous (unlike so much of the "Bambi meets Cecil B. DeMille" style that defines my Sydney peer group's decorative vision), but the house has achieved the shock value of the seductive. It is a peaceful garden oasis amid the urban sprawl of present-day Sanur.

TREASURE GROVE

THE TOURIST GHETTOS OF KUTA-LEGIAN ARE A BIT LIKE Bangkok: *kampung* (village) mayhem on the outside, with the requisite encrustations of art shops and cafés, but on the inside is the occasional oasis of exotic charm. Behind the village hall of Basang Kasa, north of Kuta, just where the trattoria belt peters out momentarily, Italian photographer Isabella Ginanneschi and her late fiancé John Read created an extraordinary garden peopled with precious pavilions and fine folk art. It is a joy to discover after braving the footpaths from hell, and a treat to explore. Part museum of Balinese building parts, part pied à terre, the compound is home to Read's unique collection of folk furniture: nineteenth-century doors from the island of Nusa Penida off Bali's south coast are set jewel-like into lofty granary facades, while delicately crafted palace windows (for tiny royals, one presumes) are resurrected as air vents in Moroccan-style niches.

It must be said here that collecting Javanese furniture has

ABOVE: MEXICO VINE (CALLED HAWAIIAN VINE IN MEXICO) COVERS THE GATE TO THE ALADDIN'S CAVELIKE COMPOUND.

RIGHT: THE TERRACE ON THE SOUTH SIDE OF THE MAIN HOUSE FEATURES A BEAUTIFUL BALINESE DOOR AND MATCHING WINDOWS FROM AN INLAND PALACE PAVILION.

112

become, in the 1990s, what the rag trade was in Kuta in the 1970s: waves and waves of fake furniture have lately washed up on the shores of the fabled isle, en route to life as an ethnic accent in the New World. Amid these tsunamis of reconstituted teak, one finds the occasional gem. Gem-spotters Read and Ginanneschi built rare collections from sorting through these piles over the past twenty years: their pixie glen of a house was their treasure grove.

The layout of the compound is basically neo-Balinese, with pavilions scattered like throw cushions in the North Legian manner. Read inherited a mangled assortment of pavilions from a former owner in 1995 and set about pulling the compound together: he added a meaningful garden with superb sculpted vistas, while simultaneously tarting up the buildings' facades with delicate architectural inserts.

It is in the interiors, however, that the house really sings, and here we see the influence of Ginnaneschi's professional background in art direction and styling: a European elegance is discernible in the clever groupings of furniture in the many petits salons. The spaces are well planned and the decorative touches whimsical—gnome-home bamboo twig hook sets vie for attention with bright aqua blue distressed Deco armchairs; uniquely carved spirit-house doors are displayed like book covers.

Even the garden bathroom with its Kuta detailing is

Mediterranean in feel: tree roots lean against the bathroom's walls of coral. Nuances from Read's beloved Mykonos can be felt in the beautiful shells laid as borders throughout the garden.

In the ordered jungle one discovers pretty niches of elegance—natural windows are cut in the hanging vines to softly frame vistas to the house temples, the *lumbung* (granary) guest house, and the kitchen kiosk. The back veranda off the main duplex pavilion opens out onto a relatively spacious lawn in the colonial tradition (it is here that one's most precious panels can be shellacked in the sun). Upstairs the master bedroom, with its attendant verandas, is stacked with juicy *objets trouvés;* the setting is straight out of *The King and I,* the governess's wing. It is quaintly Indo-Chinese, with French allure: a lacy mosquito net is settled over a Vietnamese opium bed; delicate writing chairs keep a bureau company; celadon urns on pedestal tables stand guard by the bed like Victorian chambermaids. It is an exotic and artistic tree-house space that looks out on three sides into the jungle garden.

The dashing couple—the Onassis and Maria Callas of the "Bagus Sunset" belt—crafted their dream hideaway here. It will always remain as a standard for coastal cosmopolitan chic.

LEFT: A SMALL ANTECHAMBER GREETS THE VISITOR TO THE GARDEN PAVILION BATHROOM.

BELOW: THE THRONE ROOM IN ALL ITS GLORY.

BELOW: CORAL WALLS SURROUND THE BATHROOM PAVILION.

OPPOSITE: AL FRESCO DINING IS DE RIGUEUR AT HOME IN BALI.

ABOVE: The sitting room houses many treasures from Bali, Java, and the outer islands.

LEFT: A rare collection of urns from Sambi in West Sumatra provides privacy when the service hatch is not in use.

OPPOSITE: A Mediterranean-style niche was created in one corner of the sitting room.

A GARDEN OF
PRECIOUS JEWELS

MANY YEARS AGO A BEAUTIFUL FRENCHMAN—TALL, BLOND, athletic, like actor Stewart Granger—washed up on the shores of Goa and started collecting beads. He would dress the children of the cosmic and the intense in fine raiments and paint their toes. His life as a hippie aesthete eventually led him to Bali, the world's most gorgeous culture, which beckoned with fancy dress. Here Jean-François Fichot flourished as a jeweler and a fashion plate.

Throughout the hedonistic 1970s his unique silhouette could be discerned, miragelike, raw linen flapping, on the beach at Legian, where his wares were much sought after by male peacocks and New Age princesses alike. His outfits were outrageous, his jewelry more so.

By the 1980s, hippie power-dressers from Mullumbimby to

LEFT: VIETNAMESE PLANTER POTS AND A GRACEFUL
CHAISE LONGUE DECORATE THE SPACIOUS
ENTERTAINMENT TERRACE OF THE HOUSE.

ABOVE: A BALINESE SHRINE WELCOMES GUESTS
TO THE GARDEN.

OPPOSITE: HEALTHY ANTHURIUM
LEAVES SOFTEN THE ARCHITEC-
TURE'S BALINESE FACADE.

LEFT: VIOLENT HELICONIA
FLOWERS ARE USED WITH
DEVASTATING EFFECT IN THIS
COLOR-STREWN CORNER.

RIGHT: A TERRAZZO BATHING
TUB IN THE MASTER BATHROOM.

BELOW: THE BOTANIC GARDEN
SPLENDOR OF THE GARDEN'S
LOTUS POND.

Mumbai were scrambling for his latest crystal creations. He became the most sought-after artisan on an island renowned for them. In his work he would combine decorative elements from all the different parts of his past travels. In 1990 Jean-François built his dream home across a deep ravine in the Ubud heights. Here he made a home for his collection of rare plants and other precious possessions.

Approached across a suspension bridge decorated with props from Esther Williams's classic movie, *Pagan Love Song,* the

house gate is a model of neo-Egyptian understatement—a pharoah's tomb couldn't be more discreet. Inside, the garden treasures are blinding: pulsating flaming pink anthuriums scream for attention, bright bromeliads wave lurid tongues amid sweeps of lilac-and-silver ground cover. One is surrounded by waterways, pathways, anaconda-like vines, and "opera boxes" of horticultural opulence.

On the terrace above this exotic floral stairway all is calm—a vast lily pond cools the air. Deep verandas embrace one just as they embrace huge Vietnamese planters' pots of weeping wonders.

It is a horticulturalist's dream and an asthmatic's nightmare.

Inside is really outside in Jean-François's house because the place is mostly generous verandas and open pavilions: "All the better to feed the fish, my dear," notes the megastar and host.

The color scheme of the house walls, where they exist, is vaguely Vietnamese—lemons, celadons, soft pinks—following the *Indochine* influence in the interior design (Catherine Deneuve is a demigoddess in Jean-François's pantheon). Palace-scale gilded Balinese doors and matching windows, in the florid North Bali style, are set into the walls. Mirrors, crystals, and stained glass reflect and refract the dizzying decorativeness— here a purple Tibetan pillow, there a tablescape of miniature crystal icons.

In the house's garden bathrooms Jean-François has created grottos of postmodern excess—concrete sculptural forms, glass bricks, and river boulders are used in stark contrast to the all-embracing garden elements.

Indeed "all-embracing" is a good way of describing this artistic dream home: it is a successful theatrical blend of tropical fecundity and the decorative arts.

LEFT: AN ORIENTALIST'S BOUDOIR IN THE GRAND INDO-CHINESE MANNER.

ABOVE: A PALACE DOOR CREATED BY LOCAL ARTISANS LEADS TO THE SANCTUM SANCTORUM— THE LIBRARY OF EDITH PIAF RECORDS.

AT HOME IN THE VILLAGE

VILLAGE LIFE IS THE only true life for the BALInese: temple festivals, rice harvests, and cremations are all village-run events. The village is the heart and hearth of Balinese well-being.

Villages are divided into sub-village units called *banjars,* each of which has a village hall, a *wantilan* structure, and a banjar temple. All residents of Bali are members of one banjar or another, even foreigners. The Balinese are fiercely loyal to their village deities and in most cases to their village's ruling nobles and Brahmin high priests. Few Balinese ever leave their village for good because it provides the ultimate sense of belonging, much as villages in medieval Europe used to do.

Village architecture reflects this tight-packed communalism. Village lanes are the collective living rooms; temples, the fairgrounds. The village market is the mall, and the Sunday worker bees are like the national guard. The *warung* stalls (hole-in-the-wall food outlets) are the sidewalk cafés where all gossip is collected and disseminated.

The gates of individual courtyards are left open all day, and if one is polite, one can walk through anybody's house to get to the communal land beyond. Within the house, sleeping, praying, eating, and bathing are all communal.

In a traditional house only one pavilion has a locked door and lights turned low: it is the *meten,* sometimes known as the procreation pavilion. Everything else is done under the blaze of strip neons and maximum scrutiny. In most villages there is a large open field, or *alun-alun,* around which are arranged the palace; the Temple of the Origins, or Pura Desa (*desa* means "village"); and the market. Streets and lanes run off the alun-alun, forming the village "blocks" in a rectilinear pattern. Nearly all villages are on a strong north-south axis, with some spreading east or west depending on the terrain. Even in the tourist hubs the traditional village layout and lifestyle survives behind a veneer of consumerism and the ribbons of art shops. Even busy Sanur and Kuta are model villages as far as ceremonial activities are concerned.

The earliest hostels, or *losmens,* were located in the house compounds of the villages of Kuta and Legian on the west coast, and in Ubud, in the mountains: narrow lanes opened onto generous garden compounds dotted with small huts for the guest, or *tamu,* as the paying traveler was politely known. The various kitchen, sleeping, and working pavilions of the host family surrounded the guest cottages. These early tourists got a real taste of Balinese village and family life. This tradition has continued in the housing ghettos of Kuta-Legian-Seminyak, as tourists have come back to start businesses and the village boundaries are breached by expatriate suburbs. These suburbs, the inevitable product of international tourism, have grown into exotic communities—the Italians, the Brazilians, and the Australians are particularly happy here—with great cafés serving world-class cuisine, and any number of bars and boutiques. Fruit salad and granola, the staple of yesteryear's surfies, has become sashimi, panini, or couscous as the beat has heated up. Bottle-blond Japanese boogie-boarders and aristocratic French fashion horses regularly run each other down.

The houses in these tourist ghettos are modeled on their Balinese confreres; all have romantic gardens, a sense of courtyard architecture, and masses of old Javanese furniture turning to dust.

In the upland villages, particularly in Ubud and Peliatan, foreigners often rent a corner of a family house compound and stay closely involved with the landlord's family and village activities in general. Even the luxury villas that have popped up recently in the east attach themselves to one village or another and consider themselves under the wing of some banjar or some feudal overlord. Thus the expatriates are included in the merry swirl of village life and often join in the religious life too. The Balinese are very accepting of outsiders dropping in; they might be characterized as a hippie commune with a huge cash register and a carnivorous real estate department. Famed anthropologist-writer and artist Miguel Covarrubias and his photographer wife, Rose, lived in a village in Denpasar for only a year in 1936. His book *The Island of Bali* is a remarkable treatise obviously written under the influence of his proximity to the people. Margaret Mead wrote *Character in Bali* and Walter Spies *Dance and Drama in Bali* from compounds within the warm embrace of village life, if a little on the outskirts.

The notion of setting up a satellite villa that was independent of village life came with Indonesian independence and the advent of tourism in the 1950s. With this, the dilution of the island's hard-fought autonomy had begun. Today, village boundaries are starting to blur—it is inevitable, for example, that Kuta, Sanur, and Denpasar will become one big megalopolis of rabbit-warren-like lanes and urban sprawl. Village hearts may have been run over by superhighways—even rice fields are rare in the greater Denpasar area—but, as in Mexico City, the unique spirit of the original village communities can still be felt. The processions of migrating village deities, gamelans, and devotees are bigger and bolder than ever. Village pride is on the rise. Even the expatriate communities draw lines defining hill tribes, beach blankets, Sanur snobs, and traditional white trash (the nobs in their villas).

Bali today is middle class, animistic, and fully integrated. There is no dissent. If you are Balinese, you go to the temple and take part in all the village activities. Or you leave. If you are a New Balinese, you are expected to take part in some village activities, or nobody will come if your house catches on fire. Offices and hotels function either like village banjars, through noisy consensus, or like fiefdoms with feudal overlords—the most popular model, and the one adopted by successive governments since independence. Brahmins make great teachers, the *kssatrya dewa* (warrior or ruling class) make great cops, the vil-

lagers are the worker bees, and all of us gringos buy the tickets to pay for the rides.

The Balinese believe in the philosophy of *suka-duka*—sharing the good times and the bad. Nowhere is this more evident than in the communal village life, where the turnout for a "dirty dancing" show is equal to that for an outback auntie's cremation. Among the expatriates the most interesting and exotic homes are in those tourist ghettos where *suka-duka* translates to "the agony and the ecstasy."

Village life: be in it!

HILL TRIBE HINDU
INTELLECTUAL

Diana Gude first came to Bali with a band of Australia's most famous artists—Brett Whiteley, Wendy Whiteley, and their great friend, sculptor Joel Ellenberg, Diana's fiancé. Ellenberg was in the last stages of terminal cancer and wanted to "see Bali and die." It was a very emotional time for the often sedated gang—a gaggle of hysterical actresses had gathered for the death scene, and Brett Whiteley was documenting the last throes of his last true friend.

Poet-filmmaker John Darling was helping his old chum, Ellenberg, during this difficult time, and no one was surprised when Diana stayed on "to continue her sculpting": she moved into John's charming, if frugal, retreat in the hills behind Ubud. They soon married, and Lady Di, as she became known to all of us, was within months the most informed New Balinese conservative-monarchist-animist on the block. With her gentleman aesthete she lived the life of Balinese rural bliss to the hilt: she became proficient in the Balinese language and was an active

LEFT: FIGHTING COCKS IN THE MORNING SUN.

ABOVE: A TRADITIONAL BALINESE HEARTH.

133

own studio-home in the far-flung village of Tegalsuci, near the volcano rim. The house was not called "under the volcano" but might have been, for here Diana worked, burning the midnight oil and pouring sustaining beverages into the wee hours, every night, as she wrote her highly acclaimed first novel, *The Painted Alphabet*. Her one weatherproof room was like a mobile home made from plywood and woven bamboo—a second-generation pondok retreat, with a big kitchen and numerous studio-out-houses attached. The land was terraced, generously, from its start under the broad cover of a mature banyan tree to its end, 330 feet (100 m) east, in a coffee plantation. The stepped terraces were trimmed with leafy mountain plants—moisture lovers. The dewy authoress toiled.

She gardened on Sundays, as had been the tradition in her first pondok retreat; before long we were all treated to home-made pasta flavored with mountain leaves. Expanses of well-swept compacted dirt spread out from the dining veranda, decorated only with trees and plants useful for making offerings,

member, as a married woman, of the village banjar community. Their house was upland expatriate ethnic chic as Bali had never known it before—a traditional rice-field retreat, called a *pondok* in Balinese. We all had to chew our sprouts and milk the cow.

Her life with John came to a dignified end when Darling left Bali after a fruitful career; Diana stayed on and built her like the frangipani and hibiscus. Everything was very sculptural, very refined, with a clean, cool aesthetic. Mountain breezes clipped the treetops.

Diana married again—this time with a Balinese nobleman from Ubud who had a passion for cockfighting. The courtyards were soon dotted with the distinctive woven cages the Balinese make for fighting cocks.

Today, ten years on, there is something of the Isak Dinesen about Diana as she endures bravely the writer's life of isolation in her mountain village. There may be ten thousand art shops half an hour down the newly sealed road, but here ancient spirits reign. Hers is a noble lifestyle—she has blossomed in her retrenchment.

LEFT: A LOVELY BALINESE POT, CALLED JEDING SEPI, IN THE COMPOUND'S SOUTHEAST CORNER.

BELOW: DIANA'S SCULPTURE STUDIO WITH POTAGERIE BEYOND.

A ROYAL PALACE
IN UBUD

PURI KALERAN WAS IN MANY WAYS THE FIRST OF THE "palaces" in Ubud to embrace the modern architectural style popularized by the Dutch colonial government. The outline of the present *puri* was first designed and conceived by Cokorda Rai Manuaba in the 1940s, but it has since been enhanced and has evolved to its present configuration thanks to a distinguished series of Western artists who have resided there: Hans Snel, Arie Smith, Rudolf Bonnet, Sonnega.

Many of the original buildings were inspired by the presidential palace complex in Tampaksiring, built for Sukarno in the 1950s (Corkorda Rai Manuaba was the consulting engineer for the complex). The Bale Daja was originally a conventional Balinese *bale,* which—through various additions commissioned by the resident Westerners—has evolved into its present form. The open-air bale was first enclosed with walls; then two small rooms were added onto the western end. The first artist in residence was Sonnega, who turned a series of small huts into a stu-

LEFT AND ABOVE: THE ARCHITECTURE OF PURI
KALERAN IS PART BALINESE AND PART COLONIAL.

137

dio/living room. During Hans Snel's residence (1963–1965) the kitchen and bathrooms were tacked onto the northern wall. Snel then converted the huts into a large artist's studio. The last artist to use the room for this purpose was Dutch painter Rudolf Bonnet in the 1970s.

The building is an architectural icon distinguished by its elevated base, imposing ten-foot (3 m) walls, spacious central room (the first of its kind in Ubud), and the distinctive gables of its clay tile roof. The structure was extensively renovated in the 1980s to include modern finishes and amenities which are now available and considered indispensable.

The Bale Dauh on the grounds of Puri Kaleran was from the start a building in the Western architectural tradition, and it was extensively reconfigured and modernized in the 1980s by the cur- rent resident. Its most notable inhabitant was Ubud's first doctor.

The Bale Kelod was always a rabbit warren of tiny rooms, constructed seemingly at random, which provided accommoda- tion for Cokorda Rai's numerous wives until his death in 1964. The Bale Kelod was converted into a more recognizable and functional shape in the 1970s by an eccentric French jewelry designer (he eventually left Bali because he was unable to share the limelight with Ubud's most famous artist, Jean-François.) An interesting architectural feature here is the first wood-fired pizza oven on the island. Another notable resident of the Bale Kelod was designer Linda Garland, who lived in the Bale Kelod for more than a year between houses. It was from here that La Garland designed Bali's first carved banana leaf tea tray. Shortly

after this episode, Lady Belinda Montagu restored grace and tranquillity to the grounds of the palace, collaborating with Linda Garland, her old hockey-playing chum, while working on a collection of embroidered textiles.

There is little evidence of the original gardens—in fact three frangipani trees are all that remain from the 1940s. Which is not such a bad thing, as the Balinese prefer baked earth ground swept clean every morning and evening, rather than the danger- ous liaisons occasioned by a verdant tropical garden. Gardens seem to grow through fads, much as their owners do. The cur- rent fashion is for pools, fountains, palms, and heliconia, all of which are now found spotted around the earthen court, at Puri Kaleran. The more unusual plantings found here are palms and ferns introduced from the Botanic Gardens in Sydney; Caribbean iris which surround one of the pools; and a rare orange hibiscus planted by Rudolf Bonnet.

OLD BALI
WELL PRESERVED

Tenganan is a traditional Bali Aga ("Mountain Bali") village of immense archaeological import: it is the only surviving example of the walled village type once found in many ancient Bali enclaves. It is an incredibly picturesque village famous for the beauty of its architecture and for its double-ikat ceremonial cloth, called *gringsing,* found only here and in Gujarat in India. The Tenganan villagers are admired by other Balinese for their refinement, and they speak a singsong dialect that is music to the ears.

Famed Swiss anthropologist Urs Ramseyer spent years studying the customs, art, and architecture of the village: much of his Tenganan research was published in his magnum opus *Art and Culture in Bali* (Oxford in Asia, 1979).

Closed to the outside world until the early 1960s, the village still has a secluded, exclusive feel: villagers are polite but not

ABOVE AND RIGHT: The distinctive Tenganese architecture is squat, masculine, and Zenlike in its austerity.

SEMINARY BALINESE
BAROQUE

KETEWEL VILLAGE, NEAR THE BUSY TOURIST HUB OF SANUR
on Bali's southeast coast, dates back to the tenth century, when
the area was a dense forest of teak (*ketewel* in Balinese). For at
least the last 1,000 years the village supplied the Brahmin town
of Sanur with artisans, stonemasons, and carpenters. Ketewel
tradesmen are known for their diligence, honesty, and artistic
abilities. Not surprisingly, the village has many fine temples and
some architecturally interesting *bale banjar* (community halls)
and house gates. I often use the village for architectural tours:
the still-traditional village layout—unspoiled by any high-
ways—combined with the homogeneity of the courtyard architecture make it an ideal study model.

My connection to the village is through one noble family,
descended from ennobled warriors, called *kssatrya dewa,* who
bore arms for a sixteenth-century emperor of Bali. These Dewas,
as they are known, have grown to a sizable band of fifty garden-

LEFT: THE PRIEST'S SLEEPING PAVILION AND
THE FAMILY'S HOUSE SHRINE BEYOND.

ABOVE: A VIEW INTO THE HOUSE FROM THE ENTRANCE GATE.

ers, stone-carvers, office boys, and travel guides. Their shared grandfather lives with his extended family in the Dewas' ancestral palace on the village's northern boundary. Just to the east is the famous Payogan Agung temple, where every seven months angels dance to an hypnotic gamelan beat.

Grandfather Dewa took the holy vows some years ago and now presides over his palace, called a *geria,* as a Begawan priest—that is, a high priest from a lower, non-Brahmin caste. The palace is therefore quite humble, but the ancestral temple that occupies nearly a half of the compound is a gem of Balinese temple architecture.

Visiting the geria, one always finds the priestly couple (in Bali, wives must follow their husbands into the priesthood) receiving visitors from all over the island. Devotees of the popular priest make a pilgrimage to see him and ask for an offering recipe or for a propitious date for some ceremonial activity. The saintly duo are usually sitting cross-legged on a shiny pavilion floor. Guests perch on the edge of the pavilion base; family members slouch in neighboring pavilions, weaving or reading or chatting, watching the theater of the pious across a threadbare court.

At the back of the compound, a regal backdrop to all the activities, is the magnificent house temple. Beyond the temple's low gate the priest has a magnificent library pavilion called the Gedong Saraswati after Saraswati, goddess of learning; here are kept all the holy manuscripts, religious books, and ceremonial artifacts. The rest of the shrine court is packed with pagodas and shrines. The shrines' bases are all Balinese baroque—whitewashed and deeply carved in a large scale. The resulting look is not fussy but stately. Above the bases the timber shrine boxes are tinged with powder blue and aqua; guardian demons and winged lion statues keep the deities safe.

All the walls and bases of the compound's pavilions and shrines are made from a local soapstone, called *paras,* which is quarried from the side of the river that runs through the village. Traditionally all carvings in Bali were painted or whitewashed, particularly in the royal houses: shining and other high-polish teak finishes are imports from the New World.

Water-based paint washes on decorative walls and stone carvings give a soft chiaroscuro effect—a look patented in Ketewel, the home of the cozy cornice. This priestly house is a museum of such Balinese stone carving and architectural finishes.

Two gates announce the house to the village: one is for religious processions, the other for daily use. Just inside the main gate is a miniature, very miniature, lake in the Balinese palace tradition, with an attendant cement stork. This transitional garden space quickly opens out onto the first of the three interlocking courts that make up the family home.

AT HOME IN THE PALACE

FEUDALISM SURVIVES IN BALI; MANY OF THE OLD royal families still hold sway, considerable sway, in the running of important religious festivals and the maintenance of the island's temples. Many Balinese are still "at home" in palaces of considerable grandeur, and many, many foreigners would like to be.

Sadly, most of the great palace *(puri)* compounds of the nineteenth century were burned in the first decade of the twentieth century by the royal families—Bali had nine—who refused to surrender them to the invading Dutch troops. The imperial palace in Klungkung, the old capital; the Denpasar Palace; and the Tabanan Palace were all destroyed by fire at that time. In Central Bali, the Puri Gianyar, a real jewel of a palace, survives to this day because the Gianyar royal family was more accommodating toward the colonial administration. Of the others, only the Kerta Gosa and Taman Gili pleasure gardens and pavilions of Puri Klungkung, the exquisite family house temple of the Kesiman Palace in Denpasar, and the various neglected buildings of the Puri Gede Karangasem in East Bali remain as examples of nineteenth-century palace architecture—the golden era. Picturesque roofscapes of various important buildings—drum towers, ornamental corner pavilions, and large thatched roofs of the living pavilions of the very extended families—can still be discerned in these extant puri. The palaces themselves may no longer exist, but the thick redbrick walls and handsome gates of nearly all thirty major and minor palaces still stand on the corners of Bali's larger town squares, evidence of their prominence in former times. Indeed, the palaces were prominent not just in their location but in the role they played in society. It is their patrimony, rather than any imposing scale, that lent them their majesty. Many of Bali's more famous dances, for example—the Legong and the Oleg, to name two—were invented for important events in royal palaces. The skills of goldsmiths, silversmiths, textile weavers, and artisans of every bent were kept alive by the palaces' insatiable need for fine wares.

Since at least the sixteenth century, when chinoiserie rotundas started appearing in Central Javanese palaces, the homes of the nobility have been nesting grounds for the latest trends from overseas. Hamengkubuwono I (1650–1720) of Jogjakarta, Central Java, built a magnificent Moorish-Portuguese water garden and baths, called the Taman Sari, just south of his vast multicourtyard palace. In the nineteenth and early twentieth centuries many Balinese princes returned from their European schools determined to build follies in the French or Italian manner. The magnificent water palaces they built in East Bali and West Lombok—Tirta Gangga, Taman Mayura, and Taman Narmada—can still be visited today.

In the 1920s, the king of Canton gave his trading partner, the king of Karangasem, East Bali, twenty architects, artisans, and carvers who revamped the Puri Kanginan Karangasem and many other less-documented palaces and temples. Although not a match for their very distant Indian cousins in the fort-and-palace-building department, the less wealthy rajas of Bali created gardens and temples that survive today in near mint condition.

German artist Walter Spies built the first expatriate "palace," one suspects: he invented the modified *wantilan*—a large, open, two-storied pavilion structure that has traditionally served as the community hall in all Balinese villages and is now a staple of hotel design—in order to fit his baby grand between the building's columns. His estate had sprawling spring-fed gardens, a swimming pool donated by Doris Duke, and an honor guard of spider monkeys in red-and-gold livery.

After the 1945 Indonesian Revolution of Independence, architect-president Sukarno built Pura Tampaksiring, a Deco palace on a hill above a holy temple in Central Bali, which was much copied. Art Deco had been the official style of the emerging nationalists, and Sukarno's Japanese ranch-house version, set in a vast park, influenced nobles across the island. Hundreds of historic buildings bit the dust in favor of geometric splendors.

During the 1950s and 1960s various foreigners tried to counter the growing trend toward internationalism, epitomized by the Sukarno-sponsored Hotel Bali Beach, built by the Japanese in the international school style. Antiquarian Jimmy Pandy had a legendary house on the beach in Sanur; it was crammed with palace treasures and massive floral arrangements, and had palace-scale gardens adorned with pleasure pavilions and giant statues.

Australians Warwick and Lisa Purser took up the Pandy torch in the early 1970s with lavish parties, the likes of which Bali has not seen since, in their Geoffrey Bawa–designed "palazzo." It was here that Linda Garland invented the big bamboo sofa, the Hummer of her housewares range.

Indonesian pioneers of classy tourism Wija and Tati Waworuntu followed suit when they sold their sprawling Sanur ranch to Japanese tycoon Kajima and built "Mansion House," Sanur's answer to Jackie Collins's in Bel Air. The late Dewa Manggis of Gianyar, the island's most elegant grand seigneur, laughed when he heard of the scramble for status on the coast, as he had sixteen courtyards of Murano chandeliers, crystal decanters, and a real coat of arms. Indeed the Balinese noblemen's houses always have at least four large courts with a minimum of four large pavilions, whereas the expatriate palaces rarely have more than two. It must also be said that no New Balinese party, no matter how grand, can ever rival even a minor prince's cremation or wedding for true glamour and style. But that hasn't stopped them from trying!

Palace trends in fashion, furniture, and hairdos are as much copied today as they were in the past. Since Mrs. Suharto's reign, for example, sitting room aquariums, needlepoint antimacassars, and big, thick buns of hair at the nape of the neck have been the rage across the suburbs of the land. Since the last king of Denpasar's cremation, every cremation in Bali has chosen black livery, the Denpasar royal family's house color. At a recent glamorous royal wedding in Ubud, where Megawati Sukarnoputri's choreographer and Baliophile brother Guruh was guest of honor, I counted twenty-five blonde brides of upland princes ("more upland princes than ducks," goes one popular Balinese expression) and twelve twenty-eight-inch televisions in the open reception courts. Phillip Noyce's ill-fated Bali-based feature film *The Shadow of the Peacock* (working title, "Love as Long as Your Visa Lasts") told the story of the handsome upland prince, played by John "The Last Emperor" Lone,

and his Australian bride-to-be, played by the gorgeous Wendy "Mrs. Bouvier" Hughes. *The King and I* goes grass skirt? No, but there are parallels in the home decor world. Nothing is ever going to stop thousands of horny neophytes from going the way of marble bathrooms and faux gold chandeliers; the lure of the "royal" tag is a powerful aphrodisiac. As one pundit said, "If you can't get a bionic model, you can sure buy the lounge set."

Just as Western civilization has come up with the ice cream palace, the Palais de Dance, and the People's Palace, so Balinese real estate sharks and New Age princesses have adopted the word *puri* to describe their lateral condominia and Architectural Digestible. As the real rajas have headed for the urban centers to scrape enough off of the tourism husk to maintain their numerous temples, so the pretenders have been heading for the hills, where one can secure quite large tracts of land and roll out the red carpet. Most of the results are ravishing, with incredible gardens and views. Tragically, however, it is the urban Balinese who have adopted the cheaper trappings of rajadom: the present-day capital of Denpasar is now dotted with thousands of "Louis Who" (rather than Louis XIV or XV) wannabes with black glass-and-chrome guard houses.

A WATER PALACE WITH EUROPEAN TOUCHES

CAROLE MULLER AND HER HUSBAND, ARCHITECT PETER Muller, have been a major influence throughout the last twenty-five years of Balinese architecture and interior design. In that period they fashioned the Kayu Aya on the Legian Beach (now the Bali Oberoi) for Pepsicola czar Herman Schaefer, and the Villa Ayu near Ubud (now the fabulously successful Amandari). They also redesigned Dutch painter Rudolf Bonnet's studio in Campuan, Ubud, for themselves as a hill-land retreat from their Australian homes: Marulan, a Georgian pile in the country near Canberra, and Bronte House in Bronte Park in Sydney. Carole was responsible for this writer's career, and she single-handedly invented the crocheted palm-toddy cozy, the bamboo car jack, and a patented hook (fashioned from palm leaves) for retrieving car keys locked in the car.

LEFT: CAROLE MULLER'S PALATIAL SPREAD AS VIEWED FROM THE TIRTA GANGGA GROUNDS.

ABOVE: THE CENTRAL FOUNTAIN OF THE FORMAL BALINESE GARDENS.

159

LEFT: THE LAST PRINCE OF KARANGASEM ENJOYED EXPERIMENTING WITH MODERN ARCHITECTURAL MATERIALS AND DECORATIVE METHODS, AS EVIDENCED BY THIS PRESSED CONCRETE PAVING TILE.

Her villa on the fabulous water gardens of Tirta Gangga (literally, holy water of Gangges), originally built by the last king of Karangasem in 1947, is her first solo effort in the highly competitive Balinese design stakes. In its design one sees elements of the Amandari and the Bali Oberoi—but they are here unfettered by the constraints of committees.

She has, at last, fashioned a glamorous retreat with more bottom squirters that you can poke a stick at.

"I selected the spot for its meditative views out to the Lombok straits," declares Carole. This writer noted, however, that the tranquil view is not unpleasantly interrupted by near-naked youths frolicking in the public bathing pools a petal toss

ABOVE AND RIGHT: ARCHITECTURAL ELEMENTS FROM THE ORIGINAL 1940S PALACE WERE CLEVERLY INCORPORATED INTO THE VILLA'S PLANTER BOXES.

OPPOSITE: THE VIEW FROM CAROLE'S BOUDOIR. THE DESERT ROSE PLANTS IN THE ORNAMENTAL VASES WERE HER HOMAGE TO THE FORMAL STYLE OF THE LATE PRINCE.

from the terrace. Probably a coincidence.

The original house was conceived in 1947 as a summer retreat for the Karangasem prince. It was built in the style of traditional palace architecture with a split-level *loji* pavilion, the belvedere of Balinese architecture. Carole rebuilt the walled courtyard house in 1995 using local craftsmen and running the project herself: no mercy was shown in her quest for beauty in the Balinese palace style.

The past three Karangasem rulers have been great palace builders, and Carole used many details from their combined legacy, particularly the molded cement decorative tiles and statues that the last king pioneered. She did not dismantle the touches of European-in-Asia style—the rows of weird white urns on the parapet wall, the neocolonial style of the original interiors—nor did she desert classical pavilion proportions in her search for usable space. The result is singularly Balinese but also practical for a Western lifestyle.

From every room and sitting area one surveys the broad panorama of the formal terraced water gardens; but the house is not just a viewside aerie. As one lies on either of the four-poster beds inside the main pavilion, with the cleverly mullioned glass sliding doors thrown wide open, the sound of the fountains playing below washes over one in wave after wave of bliss. It is a magical house set amid enchanting surroundings.

THE LAST OF THE RAJA'S FOLLIES

THE NINETEENTH CENTURY WAS A GOLDEN AGE FOR Balinese architecture and landscape design. The Karangasem royal family were the most prominent patrons, creating fabulous water gardens and pleasure palaces in the neighboring island of Lombok, which they ruled. The Taman Mayura and the Taman Narmada water palaces survive today as testimony to their artistic handiwork.

The royal house has also provided Balinese history with many military heroes. Since the eighteenth century at least, this far-flung kingdom has sent its young princes and princesses to the court of Prince Mangkunegara, in Solo, Central Java, for education and "finishing." (The Mangkunegara court was famed throughout Indochina for the beauty of its palace and its princesses, and for the worldliness of its well-educated ruling family.)

The young Karangasem royals would accompany the Javanese nobles on their not infrequent visits to the courts of

LEFT: THE CENTRAL FLOATING PAVILION IN THE
CHINOISERIE STYLE IN THE PALACE GROUNDS.

ABOVE: A CANTONESE-STYLE CORNER OF THE CEREMONIAL PAVILION.

167

multitiered pagoda gate as entrance to this new fantasy compound. He also experimented most successfully with a new neo-Dutch style for the sleeping pavilion in the main court: this neocolonial building, with its blazing blue Chinese doors, cast iron veranda columns, and prefab concrete decorative panels, became known as the "Bale [pavilion] Matterdam," a corruption of "Amsterdam," its inspiration. Highly ornate furniture in the same Dutch-Balinese style was created, and upholstered with thick Cantonese brocade. History records that the Dutch envoy from Batavia saw this marvel in 1933 and immediately wrote to his queen: she dispatched a beautiful fountain as a sign of her admiration.

Today the palace is barely a museum. The bones of the garden remain, as do the main pavilions and much of the furniture, but the last king left many children, and his descendants have built unsympathetic structures that encroach on the marvel and break the spell. But when discovering this heavenly hybrid for the first time, each visitor is spellbound. Hopefully one day soon all the marvels of the great architect-kings of Karangasem will be suitably restored.

Europe—to Holland in particular. The lavishly laid out gardens and chinoiserie rotundas of their European hosts fueled their fertile imaginations.

In 1920 the king of Canton, in China, heard of the Balinese king's passion for palace building and gave the Karangasem ruler a team of Chinese artisans, perhaps as a trade for troops of Legong dancers. The artisans were controlled by Encik Pow, a master architect and geomancer.

The king set the team to building Puri Kanginan, a new palace to the east of the existing main palace, the splendid Puri Gede, the grandest on the island. The new complex was to be built in the florid South Chinese style mixed with classic Balinese architectural styles. From the Solo court the king borrowed the idea of a

TOP LEFT: THE EUROPEANOISERIE FRONT PORCH OF THE BALE MATTERDAM.

LEFT: INSIDE THE BALE MATTERDAM. THE ROOMS WERE COLONIAL IN PROPORTION BUT BALINESE IN DECORATION.

OPPOSITE: THE FABULOUS BLUE CHINESE DOOR OF THE BALE MATTERDAM.

RIVERSIDE DREAM
PALACE

THIS PALACE WAS BUILT BY A FRIENDLY BAND OF EXPATRI-
ates—hardworking Australians in the big smoke of Jakarta who
wanted a glamorous Bali spread as their refuge from city life.

The development was inspired, in a very small way, by the
famous Winter Palace hotel in Luxor, which also sits on a river—
the more formidable Nile. I had visited Egypt shortly before
being commissioned to design this fun-palace and had been very
impressed by the romantic charm of Orientalist architecture. I
decided to try my hand at something Orientalist here, on a river
bend, in the pretty rice fields near the surfing beach at Canggu.
We designed Puri Canggu Mertha as a *petit palais* in a Balinese-
Moorish style emulating, perhaps, the palaces of the kings of
Karangasem, in East Bali.

I kept to a strict palette of Balinese pavilions, placed dramatically on terraces leading down to a formal pool and water

LEFT: THE MAIN ENTRANCE GATE WAS BUILT IN THE
KETEWEL VILLAGE STYLE, WITH AN INLAY OF CHINESE
PLATES PROVIDING A "RETRO" LOOK.

171

ABOVE AND RIGHT: The "moorish" swimming
pool court has elements formal, modern,
Balinese, Hindu, Chinese, and Islamic.

garden. Below the pool's edge, indeed along the property's lower line, stretches a river meander shaded by bamboo.

As our office is a Balinese design office (with one noisy New Balinese) we love to do high-kick High Balinese work, but are rarely allowed: clients in Singapore don't seem to want anything "Oriental," and in Indonesia the marketplace has been hit by a plague of butt-numbing minimalism. So it was a relief to be allowed to do what we do best—architecture that looks as if it's an excuse for a fabulous garden.

Puri Canggu Mertha is a series of garden surprises, encountered through a series of well-dressed Balinese gates. I say "well-dressed" because great care was taken to give every gate a unique and glamorous look, befitting its role: there are two quite imposing entrance gates into the north and south quarters of the compound, and some ten individualized house gates for the various villa, pool, and pond experiences. On many of the gates I used a Balinese belle epoque chinoiserie decorative trick—embedding plates, like medallions, in the brickwork. Antique doors, of many subtle hues, were used in every gate—antique carved panels were copied and enlarged as large air vents and decorative outriders for the aristocratic gates.

The property is a *puri* (palace) in pretension only—no nobles displaced here—so the interiors, also by my office, are colorful but not over-the-top grand like so many post-tourist-boom palaces across the land. The property has dignity, a dignity that comes from suitable design. In the detailing—in the notion of a palace borrowing from other lands—we tried to inject some glamour. In the main salon giant Chinese winged lions, illuminated by Arts and Crafts chandeliers made from Javanese architectural pieces, peer down from partition walls. The communal pavilion's columns, modeled on federation house columns in Australia, fuse in a natural way with Balinese pavilion architecture. Rich wall finishes by Australian artist Stephen Little, and statues, add "oomph" to the stolid pavilion form. The gardens are quite exuberant: the landscape design has become the interior decoration, as is so often the case in Bali.

Both pool courts borrow freely from Peter Muller's floating pool pavilion at the now-famous Amandari Hotel near Ubud in Central Bali; the "winter palace" pool area has an adjacent formal water garden and pergola.

Since 1998 Puri Canggu Mertha has become a rental property. Waves of paradise-seekers now waft through. Quite often they remark that they've discovered the real Bali inside the hotel's gate. For our design team, that is the ultimate compliment.

MERLIN'S FOLLY
OPPOSITE THE DISCO
ON THE BEACH
(A LOVING PORTRAYAL)

MILO GAVE BALI THE JERSEY TANK TOP. IN ALL COLORS. HE reintroduced Lurex to a populace starved for glamour and *la dolce vita*. His first house, vast by 1970s standards, in the rice fields south of the Bali Oberoi, was likened to the Emerald City of *The Wizard of Oz*—everything gleamed and glittered, everyone was young and beautiful, even the pet gorillas had diamonds in their teeth. His vast octagonal pagoda, the starship for his enterprise, had everything. There were marble grapes dripping from the ceiling—in all colors; mother-of-pearl terrazzo bathrooms—in all colors; and a phantasmagorical first floor, part *Barbarella,* part Diana Vreeland, part Karate Kid. Milo's car was speckled gold to match his hair; he took his position as senior wizard seriously. He was devout in making Balinese offerings and

ABOVE AND LEFT: THE PRIVATE SALON OF THE ORIENTALIST
PAGODA WITH ITS HAUTE CHINOISE ACCENTS.

LEFT: MILO PIONEERED THE
SHELL INLAY PLASTER NOW
POPULAR ALONG THE FUN
BUM BELT.

RIGHT: INSIDE MILO'S PAGODA
THE ARCHITECTURAL FINISHES
ARE RICHLY DECORATIVE.

BELOW: AN 18TH-CENTURY
JAVANESE PEDESTAL TABLE AND
TWO COLONIAL CANE CHAIRS.

credit for the lime green and purple Moscow Subway House gate, with inset Shiva, or the Tarzan dip pool adjacent the high church shrine, or Momma's anthurium collection. "Over the top" would be an understatement, but Milo's realized dreams are not showy: like the man, they are a subtle blend of strong beliefs—in the house's case, architectural conviction and passion for decoration. Milo loves to decorate: his work is always beautifully researched and crafted. Indonesian textile patterns are his passion—and he and Linda Garland are the only two expatriates of their generation to be asked by the Indonesian Department of Trade to advise on local skills and trades.

The new pagoda, minus the monkeys and peacocks and the streams of disciples, is a luxurious retreat for a master craftsman, an artist who has brought new vision and direction to his adopted home.

a trendsetter in the styles stakes: if Milo wore rainbow diapers, all Kuta followed suit. He was a perfectionist in everything he did. (He cooked perfect pasta that was organic "nuclear" fusion.)

When after twenty years the lease ran out on his palace, a black hole was poised to appear in the pantheon of expatria. What next? Was it to be a phoenix from the ashes? A brave new face? No, he amazed everyone by cloning the 1960s marvel-mansion, albeit with a charming *Indochine*/Moghul Empire face-lift, and was soon open again for the business of dispensing charms and influencing people. The new pagoda in Kuta is "more stargazer's astrodome than Merlin's cave," Milo explains. It was realized with the help of rising star architect Anak Agung Yokasara. This writer advised on the planting and general landscape but will not take

STYLISH HOSPITALITY
AND DISCREET PAVILIONS

Adrian Zecha is the godfather of all Aman hotels; he has elevated the words "clean, spacious, and stylish" to the pantheon of the precious. His name is synonymous with elegant hospitality and great architecture. It is only fitting that his Bali house should be a monument to gracious living.

In 1985 Ed Tuttle (designer of the Amankila in Bali, the Amanpuri in Thailand, the Amanjiwo in Central Java, and the Amangawi in the United States) was called in to revamp the legendary Donald Friend estate, which Zecha had acquired in a poker game from award-winning Sanur developer Wija Waworuntu. Donald Friend had been the great white raja of Batu Jimbar estates for two decades. Lovingly known as Tuan Donal', he inspired a generation of escape artists and built many beautiful homes along the beach. His last house, built after his vast land-

ABOVE AND RIGHT: Australian artist Donald Friend commissioned a Sri Lankan architect to build a museum to house his collection of bronzes and other Balinese art. Adrian Zecha, with designer Ed Tuttle, added the romanesque poolscape.

holdings were subdivided into a real estate development, was on a one-acre beachside plot: it had a fantastic studio/living quarters. The romantic gardens, strewn with follies, were one of the wonders of modern Bali. In 1975 famed Sri Lankan architect Geoffrey Bawa designed various additions to the house, including a large museum building to house Friend's impressive collection of Bronze Age artifacts and Balinese artworks. In 1985 Friend left the island, and the house was leased to Adrian Zecha, an Indonesian by birth with a brilliant international career. Tuttle's 1989 renovation of Bawa's upgrade gave the estate a whole new look, but sadly, Sanur's most beautiful romantic garden was destroyed in the process. Tuttle and Zecha wanted a "clean, spacious, and stylish" look compatible with their vision for a new, organized tomorrow. They wanted perspectives, not romantic excess. Hundreds of square meters of Linda Garland–championed apricot-blush concrete were poured over coral garden pavers and tender terraces; bodies were carved on the scattered Buddha relics; and a pool court was added with a Balinese temple top like a tea cozy for the pump room. A great carver was commissioned to do a mural of a Balinese procession stretching 160 feet (50 m) in the entrance gallery. Beyond was Tuttle's clever main house gate and metal detector, both Majapahit style and Aryan architectonic. Joyce Marr, Hong Kong's answer to Diana Vreeland, booked the premises for her conversion to Confucianism, Fergie had a tryst there: indeed, for many years Adrian and Bebe Zecha received the world graciously from their understatedly elegant holiday home. And the world came, and they marveled at the things in rows, and there was one cold beer each.

The house's most charming areas even today, after the

OPPOSITE AND LEFT: THE FLOORS WERE DONE WITH A LOCAL TERRAZZO FINISH, POPULAR SINCE DUTCH COLONIAL TIMES.

RIGHT: THE INSIDE OF THE MUSEUM BUILDING FEATURED 19TH-CENTURY CARVED BALINESE PANELS AS CUPBOARD DOORS AND NICHES FOR STATUARY AND ART PIECES.

Zechas' time, are not the museum's mezzanine or the poolside plaza, nor Friend's old sitting room, now revamped and very chic, but two discreet pavilions tucked into the beachside part of the property—one raised, one sunken into a large lotus pond.

The raised dining pavilion is turned away from the strict linear access of the palace-scale Balinese courtyard toward the magnificent views of the straits of Bali and the island of Nusa Lembongan beyond. The super-thin pavilion columns are elegantly carved and colored to match a decorative panel at the roof's apex. Lunch was served by the Zechas on celadon plates with black place mats and silver chopsticks. A row of five ancient *tempayan* vats sits against the wall in the plaza-ette behind the pavilion.

The sunken floating sitting pavilion, with its apricot-blush cement "strobate" base, is the Tuttle renovation's pièce de résistance, modeled on cockfighting pavilions in Outer Mongolia. The tiered floor was designed in such a way that one's eyes are at water level, with the field of strident pink lotuses literally in one's face.

It was at the Zecha palace that the international playboy Hugo Jesseriati invented the basket of stiff tuberoses for Interflora Sanur; it was here that Yoko Ono first dropped her face furniture in an effort to see the Hon. Basil Charles doing the Watusi with heiress Idanna Pucci; it was here that the two

LEFT AND RIGHT: THE MAIN SITTING ROOM ROUGHLY FOLLOWS THE LINES OF THE "WANTILAN" PAVILION WHERE DONALD FRIEND LIVED AND PAINTED. ED TUTTLE'S SOFAS COMPLEMENT OTHER GIANT SEATING PODS BUILT INTO "BAYS" BETWEEN THE COCONUT WOOD COLUMNS.

BELOW: A LOUNGING NICHE WITH ITS OWN LILY POND COURTYARD.

giant bamboo orchestras from West Bali played simultaneously, for the first time, to a packed house of celebrities.

The house has had many lives and seen many parties and distinguished visitors. After being just an often empty shell with a few loyal retainers rattling around in the old playground of Tuan Donal', during the Zecha interregnum the house was considered the grandest house in Bali, albeit a tad forbidding.

ABOVE: THE SUNKEN SITTING
ROOM IN THE LOTUS POND—
TUTTLE'S PIÈCE DE RÉSISTANCE
OF THE 1989 RESTORATION.

LEFT: A DETAIL OF THE CARVED
STELE LAMPS PARKED IN
THE CORNERS OF THE LOTUS
PAVILION.

RIGHT: ONE OF THE COM-
POUND'S MANY DECORATIVE
TEMPAYAN GLAZE POTS FROM
THE AGE OF CHINESE TRADE.

OPPOSITE: THE ORNAMENTAL
CORAL GATE, IN THE KORI
AGUNG STYLE OF BALINESE
PALACE GATES, ACTS AS A NOBLE
BACKDROP FOR THE LOTUS
PAVILION'S MAIN VISTA.

AT HOME FOR THE GODS

THERE ARE TENS OF THOU- SANDS OF VILLAGE deities in Bali; many are the dei- fied ancestors of royal fam- ily members. These gods dwell in the numerous vil- lage temples or family house shrines; all the temples are walled garden compounds with separate shrine buildings. The higher, more ancient Balinese gods live in the crater lakes and the island's three volcanic peaks. The gods of the Hindu holy trin- ity—Brahma, Shiva, and Vishnu—have separate temples in the vast, sixty-four- temple complex, Pura Besakih, called the Mother Temple, which is situated in the foothills of the metaholy Mount Agung.

All Balinese temples are incredibly beautiful; even trends toward prefabri- cated, garage rooftop, and canned gold-leaf temples have not destroyed the uniqueness and picturesqueness of these homes for the gods. And homes they truly are, for the gods' palaces, or pura, have spring cleaning rites, housewarming ceremonies, and even audience halls and reception rooms for gods visiting from neighboring villages. Among the thousands of pura are six Pura Agung, or state temples, which have "time-share apartments," as it were, in all the island's village temples: here higher deities—those of the crater lakes, the mountains, and the holy springs—may at any time descend and take up occupancy. These high-rise shrines are represented as *meru*, or pagodas, with black thatched roofs fashioned from *ijuk* fiber. (Ijuk fiber comes from the trunk of the sugar palm tree, which is considered more holy than the coconut because of its extra height.)

The original worshiping grounds of the ancient Balinese in the mountains were terraced sanctuaries; many mountain temples today still exhibit this early form. Cairns of rocks, monoliths, and crouched figures symbolizing fertility were found in these ancient pura in Bali, as indeed they were found across the Asia-Pacific region, as far east as Hawaii and the New Hebrides.

With the arrival of Buddhism in the ninth century, meditation caves and monasteries appeared on the banks of Central Bali's holy river, the Petanu, and stupas and *chedi* domes were built over ancient worshiping grounds. With the arrival of the classic Hindu culture in the tenth century, lingam (male) and yoni (female) stones and funerary statues commemorating deified kings and queens were added to the existing temple forms and pavilions. South Indian architectural elements—*gapura* gates and *candi* shrines—were also added to the picture book of temple elements during this period of colonization by conversion.

If we look at Balinese temple buildings, with their slightly upturned roofs and abundance of red-and-gold decoration, we detect a strong Chinese influence too. *Padma-sari* altars to the sun god, which are found in every Balinese temple, are built resting on turtle figures entwined with two snakes—evidence of crossbreeding with Chinese religious philosophy and temple form. (There was much trade between China and Indonesia during the first millennium A.D.; and until the twentieth century the Indonesian region was included in the geographic region called Indochina.)

In the larger, multicourtyard Balinese temples we see evidence of early South Indian Hindu temples, with their stone vaults and towering gates. We also find a little of the pixieland prettiness of the courtyards of Vietnam's former capital, Hue, the Fragrant City, and pavilion structures similar to those in Sri Lanka and in Kerala, India. All of Bali's late-Hindu-period temples (seventeenth and eighteenth centuries) are descended from Central and East Javanese models: this classic Hindu Javanese temple architecture was introduced to Bali by priests and noblemen who arrived in waves, ahead of the Islamization of Java around the sixteenth century. The Balinese ability to adopt, adapt, and absorb is nowhere more evident than in their homes for the gods.

With the Javanese model came the forbidden baths for the princesses, the sunken temple pond for the magical albino salamanders (a must in any worshiping ground of quality), and the stone pagodas, or *prasada,* with their slender bodies, which grace a few very lucky temples in South Bali.

The temple architecture varies considerably throughout the island. During Dutch colonial times, when Singaraja, on the north coast, was the island's capital, many studies were done of the fabulously florid temples of this region. The use of such terms as High Gothic or rococo would not be incorrect in describing these fanciful forms, often realized in painted pink soapstone. The temples also exhibit Chinese and colonial influence in their door carvings and outbuildings.

The temples in the south, by comparison, are stolid and handsome. They are generally made entirely of red brick, after the style of the Majapahit empire of East Java, which had so influenced South Bali.

In Central Bali, particularly in the Ubud and Gianyar districts, the temples are built of gray soapstone or an ornate mix of gray soapstone and red brick. In the Dalem temples, near the graveyard, the decoration verges on the phantasmagorical—stone effigies of long-nailed witches, ogres, and spooks are added to remind devotees of the origins of these temples as worshiping grounds for Kali, the goddess of death.

In East Bali the style is elegant and squat; there is less deep carving and a general respect for simplicity of line and grace of proportion. In the mountain temples bright, painted finishes replace carved stone, as the volcanic rock in mountain areas is less suitable for carving. The mountain temples look quite Chinese, as do the mountain folk, descended as they are from the earliest migrations from South China and the hill tribes of the Golden Triangle region (the Hmong, the Akah, and the Dai).

Not only do Balinese gods have homes, but they also have holidays, "beach resorts," and "honeymoon hotels"—the liaisons of the various deities are as much a topic of reverential gossip among the priests as are the goings-on among the less ethereally inclined. The beach resorts are the Pura Segara, temples to the sea god, Baruna; here village gods go once a year to bathe in the sea and partake of the elixir of life, *tirta amerta,* made from churning the eternal ocean.

Temples provide a great opportunity for village social activity too. "Heavy petting in a temple setting" is a no-no, but the Lurex sashes and ylang-ylang headdresses that teenage girls adorn themselves with are powerful magnets for village youth. Entrancing, too, are the Barong dances and clashing metallophones for the babies, and the fairground games in the forecourt for the gamblers. Trance sessions and sacred dances provide entertainment for the devout. The Balinese are not precious about their religion— beauty, fun, and games are built into most events.

BALI'S MOST BEAUTIFUL ROYAL CHAPEL

OVER FIVE HUNDRED YEARS AGO THE CLASSIC ARCHITEC-tural style of the Hindu empires of East Java was introduced into Bali. Via palaces and temple buildings the style, named Majapahit after the last golden empire of Hindu Java, quickly took root—it became the predominant architectural style and has survived fairly intact in temples and palaces to this day. One has to search out unspoiled examples of domestic courtyards, however, as the Suharto era of rococo hedonism saw a plum-meting in respect for local culture among the ruling families and other assorted elite.

One survivor is the Merjan Puri Kesiman, the Royal Chapel of the Kesiman Palace in Denpasar, once Bali's most artistic and admired. It was designed as a moated garden temple by a disciple of the great priest-architect Dwijendra in the eighteenth century.

Architecturally, the grandeur of the stone pagodas and the tightness and classical beauty of the complex's guardian statues

LEFT AND ABOVE: The MAGNIFICENT RED BRICK KORI AGUNG gate in classic 18TH-CENTURY STYLE ANNOUNCES THE ROYAL CHAPEL PROPER FROM ACROSS THE MOAT.

are without peer on the island. One must go to the inner sanctum of the doge's palace in Venice, one fantasizes, to find an architectural gem of such Byzantine beauty.

Every six months, at the time of the temple's anniversary rites, the pagodas and shrines are adorned with brocade buntings and "eave earrings" fashioned from coconut palm leaves; gilt umbrellas, the palace standards, and other palladia dress up the architecture. The altars and elaborate spirit houses are piled high with silver trays of magnificent fruit offerings.

The god of the temple, the deified spirit of an illustrious ancestor represented by a golden deer (the symbol of the Majapahit empire) is then taken to the temple dedicated to the island's most beloved saint, Dwijendra, at Uluwatu, on a perch high above the crushing waves of the Indian Ocean. Upon the deity's return from its holy pilgrimage, a water buffalo is sacrificed on the brick bridge that leads to the temple gate, itself a copy of the great gate at Uluwatu, one of the island's most beautiful.

The Roman bricks of Majapahit style have here been fashioned with a very gentle hand indeed: the decoration on the shrine bases is subdued, deferring, as it were, to the various statues and handsome urns that dot the ornamental temple-garden-court. Every day, almost hourly, village maidens and members of the royal family place delicate offerings at the statues' bases and at the mouth of the redbrick shrines. These daily processions of devotion confirm the position the house still holds in the community, now a middle-class suburb of East Denpasar. They also add essential daily ritual to the static beauty of the temple complex.

RIGHT: THE INDIVIDUAL PAVILIONS AND SHRINES WITHIN THE "TEMPLE" COMPLEX ARE SEPARATED BY BODIES OF WATER—THE COMBINATION OF ORNATE ARCHITECTURE AND NARROW STRIPS OF WATER IS MORE LIKE VENICE THAN ANY INDIAN MOGUL MODEL.

HOUSE TEMPLES AND SHRINES ACROSS BALI

BALI HAS NOT ONLY MANY AND VARIED TEMPLE COMPLEXES but also private shrines and niches found in courtyards across the land. These can be temporary structures, fashioned out of split bamboo or tree branches, or simple spirit-house-like brick shrines, for the spirit of the land. In mountain villages one finds elaborately carved and painted altars to the sun god Surya, or to the supreme deity, Acintya.

The existence of these picturesque shrines, often flanked by frangipani trees or hibiscus bushes, in a courtyard home is really what makes a Balinese garden Balinese. A gathering of shrines in the corner of a courtyard home is called a *sanggah,* or family house temple. It is here that the spirit of every Balinese returns, after elaborate rituals that ensure the soul's graduation to a semi-

TOP: THE SWASTIKA IS THE SYMBOL OF THE ISLAND'S HINDU-BUDDHIST FAITH.

RIGHT: THE MULTIDISCIPLINARY SHRINE OF FASHION MOGUL MILO COVERS ALL BASES—TIBETAN BUDDHIST, BALINESE ORTHODOX, AND CHINESE.

divine state. Bali is known as Pulau Dewata, or Island of the Semidivine Non-Underworld Ancestor Spirits. It's a long story, lost in the mists of time, but the ancient Indonesian spirit worship seems to have acquired all the juiciest bits, architecturally and philosophically, of Chinese ancestor worship and classic Hindu religion. The family house shrine has evolved architecturally into an outdoor Chinese altar table with elements of Oriental ornamental (the finials, top knots, and gaily painted spirit houses). Philosophically it has evolved into a place of pantheistic worship; worship of the Hindu holy trinity and the moon goddess, to name just the upper crust, and of all the clan group's ancestor spirits.

During the Balinese all saints' season, called Galungan-Kuningan, ancestor spirits descend into the *sanggah,* which always occupies a sizable plot in the northeastern corner of the compound. The statue garden of mossy shrines then becomes a fairground of colored umbrellas, fanciful buntings, woven decorations, and bolts of white, yellow, and checkered cloth wrapped around the shrines' waists.

Most of the island's single shrines (that is, those outside the family house temple) receive blessings and offerings at least three times a day, at the completion of each rice-cooking session. As a result, the shrines generally appear adorned with flowers and incense, and flanked by the occasional canine waiting for his next snack.

Indeed, one of the great experiences of Bali is to come across a mossy shrine in the rice fields, or a spirit house under a giant banyan tree, alive with fresh flower offerings and burning sticks of incense.

Niches are also fashioned into house gates, and on ceremonial building walls: almost every pavilion or room in Bali (the bathroom being the exception) has a small altar shelf, called a *plangkiran,* placed high in its northeast corner. These receive daily offerings and major blessings at the full moon and on other holidays.

OPPOSITE: SHANE SWEENEY PAINTED THIS BUDDHA THANGKA IN THE STYLE OF ARTIST MARTIN SHARP'S LEGENDARY JIMI HENDRIX POSTER.

ABOVE: MOST PAVILIONS ON THE ISLAND HAVE A SMALL ALTAR WHERE DAILY OFFERINGS ARE MADE.

RIGHT: A SIMPLE SANGGAH
CUCUK OR TEMPORARY SHRINE.

FAR RIGHT: A PADMA-SARI WITH
ATTENDANT WHITE-OVER-GOLD
UMBRELLA.

BELOW: A SPIRIT HOUSE SHRINE
CALLED A BEDUGUL, DEDICATED
TO THE SPIRIT OF THE LAND,
IS FOUND IN EVERY HOUSE
COMPOUND.

BELOW LEFT: A SHRINE IN A
MOUNTAIN COURTYARD.

BELOW RIGHT: THE PADMA SARI
AT DENPASAR'S SAGAT NATA
TEMPLE.

BOTTOM: THE PADMA-SARI
ALWAYS SITS IN THE NORTHEAST
CORNER OF THE HOUSE COM-
POUND'S COURTYARD.

OPPOSITE: A SMALL VOTIVE
STATUE FROM JAVA'S CLASSICAL
HINDU ERA.

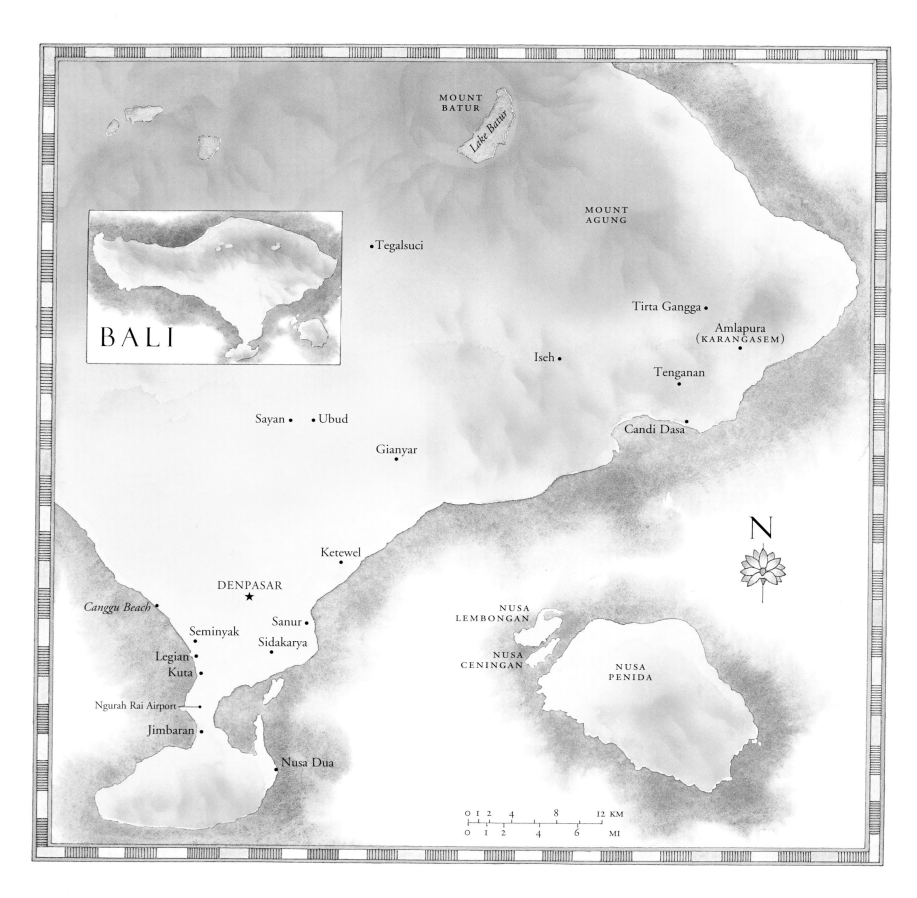

MOUNT
BATUR

Lake Batur

MOUNT
AGUNG

• Tegalsuci

Tirta Gangga •

Amlapura
(KARANGASEM)

Iseh •

Tenganan
•

BALI

Sayan • • Ubud

Candi Dasa
•

Gianyar
•

N

Ketewel
•

DENPASAR
★

NUSA
LEMBONGAN

Canggu Beach •

Sanur •

NUSA
CENINGAN

NUSA
PENIDA

Seminyak

Sidakarya
•

Legian
Kuta •

Ngurah Rai Airport —•

Jimbaran •

Nusa Dua
•

0 1 2   4   8   12 KM

0 1 2   4   6   MI

VISITOR'S GUIDE

MUSEUMS

BALI MUSEUM
Jalan Letkol Wisnu, Denpasar
Phone: (0361) 222680
Designed as a Balinese palace, it houses an eclectic collection from Bali's prehistoric age through its late classical period.

GUNARSA MUSEUM OF CLASSICAL BALINESE ART
Jalan Pertigaan Banda
Banjarangkan, Klungkung
Phone: (0366) 22256
The three-story museum adjacent to artist Nyoman Gunarsa's eccentric studio/home features a fine collection of classical Balinese paintings, sculptures, carvings, and architectural elements. See the private zoo and sculpture garden at the museum's back.

LE MAYEUR MUSEUM
Jalan Hang Tuah, Sanur
Phone: (0361) 286201
Former home of the legendary 1950s loverboy, Impressionist Le Mayeur. This idyllic beachside bungalow offers a glimpse into the life of a Bali-besotted artist/aristocrat.

MUSEUM NEKA, SANGGINGAN
Jalan Raya Sanggingan
Campuhan, Ubud
Phone: (0361) 975074
Bali's most comprehensive collection of late 20th century Balinese art, by foreign artists too. Impresario Suteja Neka was a driving force behind the art market during the formative years of Balinese tourism.

PURI LUKISAN MUSEUM OF BALINESE PAINTING
Jalan Raya Ubud, Ubud
Phone: (0361) 975136
Founded by Dutch painter Rudolf Bonnet under the auspices of Cokorda Sukawati, and set in picturesque grounds, the museum has a permanent collection and regular retrospectives of famous Balinese artists.

TAMAN BURUNG, BIRD PARK
Jalan Raya Batubulan
Singapadu, Gianyar
Phone: (0361) 299352
In 1996 German jeweler Eddy Swadarbo exercised his twin passions—collecting birds and making gardens—in this superb five-acre park of tropical wonders.

TEMPLES OPEN TO THE PUBLIC
(Temple Attire Required)

PURA BESAKIH
Desa Besakih, Karangasem
The "Mother Temple," this terraced sanctuary of vast courts and imposing pagodas dates from the 11th century.

PURA LUHUR
Uluwatu, Ungasan
A cliff-top temple of amazing beauty, overlooking the Indian Ocean.

PURA MAOSPAHIT
Jalan Sutomo
Denpasar
This 16th-century state temple was built in the massive brick course-work style imported to Bali with the Hindu migration from the East Javan Majapahit empire.

PURA PENATARAN AGUNG
Pejeng, Gianyar
Home of the famed 2,000-year-old "Neraka," the world's largest bronze kettle drum.

PURA SAMUAN TIGA
Bedulu, Gianyar
This striking temple complex outside Ubud is also historically important; here, in the 14th century, the various ancient clans of central and mountain Bali formed Bali's first pan-island pact.

PURA TAMAN AYUN
Mengwi, Tabanan
Pretty moated temple complex on the road to Sangeh, the Monkey Forest.

PURA TANAH LOT
Tabanan
Famed fairy-tale temple on a rock near a golf course designed by Greg Norman and a Suharto-era hotel complex.

PURA TIRTA EMPUL
Tampaksiring, Gianyar
One of the holiest temples in Bali, it sits in a verdant valley behind Indonesia's presidential summer palace and has a sacred spring.

PALACES AND PALACE GARDENS OPEN TO THE PUBLIC

PURI KANGINAN
Jalan Sultan Agung
Amlapura, Karangasem
Whimsical palace of pavilion follies built in the Chinese and European styles. See pages 166–69.

PURI SAREN AGUNG
Jalan Raya Ubud
Ubud
Phone: (0361) 975057
Fax: (0361) 975137
Palace of the late Cokorda Agung Sukawati, prince of Ubud, who—with famous German artist Walter Spies—founded the Pita Maha art movement.

TAMAN KERTA GOSA
Jalan Surapati
Klungkung
Eighteenth-century pleasure gardens surrounding the beautiful pavilions of the palace of Klungkung, in the former imperial capital of Bali.

TAMAN UJUNG
Ujung, Amlapura, Karangasem
Ruins of last king of East Bali's palatial water gardens, built in 1936.

TIRTA GANGGA
Amlapura, Karangasem
Formal water garden and temple complex of the king of East Bali. Sister to Taman Ujung's Europeanoiserie style. See pages 158–63.

PURI AGUNG WISATA
Kerambitan, Tabanan
Phone: (0361) 812667
Fax: (0361) 810662
Formerly known as Puri Kerambitan; now offering rooms for tourists under the new name. One of Bali's last surviving palaces in the classical architectural style.

HOTELS WITH NOTABLE ARCHITECTURE AND GARDENS

AMANDARI HOTEL
Sayan, Ubud
Phone: (0361) 975333
Fax: (0361) 975335
Twenty-seven walled garden suites built to re-create a Balinese village.

BALI OBEROI
Jalan Kayu Aya
Seminyak
Phone: (0361) 730361
Fax: (0361) 730791
Australian architect Peter Muller's seminal, pivotal boutique hotel, built in 1972.

FOUR SEASONS RESORT JIMBARAN
Jimbaran
Phone: (0361) 701010
Fax: (0361) 701020
The island's most glamorous; spectacular gardens.

LA TAVERNA
Jalan Danau Tamblingan No. 29
Sanur
Phone: (0361) 288497
Fax: (0361) 287126

The Machetti brothers, Italian impresarios in Hong Kong, built this charming village-style hotel in the 1970s.

PEMECUTAN PALACE HOTEL
Jalan M. H. Thamrin No. 2
Denpasar
Phone: (0361) 423491
The handsome palace home and hotel of the still powerful prince of Denpasar.

PURI CANGGU MERTHA
Jalan Pengubungan, Banjar Silayukti
Canggu, Kerobokan
Phone: (0361) 411388
Fax: (0361) 411388
Village-style hotel with classical Balinese gardens. See pages 170–175.

TAMAN BEBEK
Sayan, Ubud
Phone: (0361) 975385
Fax: (0361) 976352
Cottages in the garden of the late, great musicologist Colin McPhee. See pages 42–47.

TANJUNG SARI
Jalan Danau Tamblingan No. 41
Sanur
Phone: (0361) 288441, 286595
Fax: (0361) 287930
Local home to kings and rock stars from 1970 to the present day. Winner of the prestigious Aga Khan Award in 1993.

SOURCE GUIDE

IN BALI

ANTIQUES, TEXTILES

AGUS SHOP
Jalan Basangkasa No. 44
Basangkasa, Kuta
Phone: (0361) 753236

ANANG'S ART SHOP
Jalan Bypass Ngurah Rai No. 3x
Tuban, Kuta
Phone: (0361) 755281

AULIA
Jalan Tunjung Makar 176
Kuta
Phone: (0361) 732479

BALI GONG ART
Batuan, Sukawati
Gianyar
Phone/Fax: (0361) 298269

BALI SOUVENIR
Jalan Raya Kerobokan No. 112
Br. Taman, Kerobokan
Kuta
Phone: (0361) 731445

LAWAS OLD TEAK FURNITURE
Jalan Raya Kerobokan
Banjar Taman, Kerobokan
Kuta
Phone: (0361) 733272
Fax: (0361) 733273

LILY FURNITURE
Antique Interior
Jalan Kayu Aya No. 99x
Oberoi, Kerobokan
Phone: (0361) 730054
Fax: (0361) 730811

PELANGI TRADITIONAL WEAVING
Jalan Soka No. 48
Denpasar
Phone: (0361) 462689

POLOS GALLERY
Jalan Legian Kelod
Kuta
Phone: (0361) 752410
Fax: (0361) 751218

PT. BUSANA INDAH
Jalan Legian Kaja No. 502
Kuta
Phone: (0361) 751185
Fax: (0361) 751911

WIRAS
Jalan Pantai Kuta
Kuta
Phone: (0361) 753253

DESIGN SHOWROOMS, HOUSEWARES

BAMBOO FOUNDATION
Br. Nyuh Kuning
Desa Mas, Ubud
P.O. Box 196
Ubud 80571
Phone/Fax: (0361) 974027

GAYA INTERIORS
Jalan Danau Poso
Sanur
Phone: (0361) 286931

JENGGALA CERAMICS
Jalan Uluwatu No. 2
Jimbaran
Phone: (0361) 703310, 703311

KAYA GAYA
Jalan Raya Seminyak
Seminyak, Kuta
Phone: (0361) 731132

PESAMUAN CERAMICS
Jalan Pungutan No. 25
Sanur
Phone: (0361) 281440

WIJAYA CLASSICS
Jalan Bypass Ngurah Rai
Pesanggaran, Denpasar
Phone: (0361) 720946
Fax: (0361) 720507

BOUTIQUES

BIASA
Jalan Raya Seminyak No. 36
Kuta
Phone: (0361) 730945
Fax: (0361) 730766

DARGA GALLERY
Kompleks Sanur Raya
Jalan Bypass Ngurah Rai Nos. 20-21
Denpasar
Phone: (0361) 285249
Fax: (0361) 285363

THE GALLERY AND BOUTIQUE AT THE FOUR SEASONS RESORT JIMBARAN
Jimbaran
Phone: (0361) 701010
Fax: (0361) 701020

MILO'S
Kuta Square
Kuta
Phone: (0361) 754081

WARISAN ANTIQUES
Jalan Raya Padang Luwih
Banjar Tegal Jaya
Dalung, Kuta
Phone: (0361) 421752
Fax: (0361) 421214

OUTSIDE BALI

(All of the following carry Balinese antiques; from time to time some may also offer textiles and contemporary items.)

U.S.A.

WARISAN
7470 Beverly Boulevard
Los Angeles, CA 90036
Phone: (323) 938-3960
Fax: (323) 938-3959

DAVID SMITH & CO. ANTIQUES
334 Boren Street North
Seattle, WA 98109
Phone: (206) 223-1598

BRUCE FRANK
215 West 83rd Street
New York, NY 10024
Phone: (212) 595-3746

TUCKER ROBBINS
366 West 15th Street
New York, NY 10011
Phone: (212) 366-4427

ETHNIC DESIGN
53 N.E. 40th Street
Miami, FL 33137
Phone: (305) 573-8118

EUROPE

LOMBOK
4 Heartmans Road
London SW6
U.K.
Phone: (0171) 736-5171

JEROME ABEL SEGUIN
36 rue Etienne Marcel
Paris 75002
France
Phone: (1) 42 21 37 70

ASIA/PACIFIC

BOW WOW
1093 Barrenjoey Road
Palm Beach, Sydney
Australia
Phone: (2) 9974 1762

PLANTATION COLONIAL TRADING CO.
3 Leura Avenue
Claremont, Perth
Australia
Phone: (08) 93 83 29 44

TANGLIN SHOPPING CENTRE
(antique shops)
Tanglin Road at Orchard Road
Singapore

INDEX

213

I would like to acknowledge all the people who invited me to enjoy their magical homes, and the Balinese people who make everything uncomplicated with their smiles.

Special thanks to my friend Linda Garland for her trust during difficult times. To my agent, Jayne Rockmill, for her caring help. To Abbeville Press for publishing my first book, and to Patricia Fabricant for her kind collaboration. And to my family for their endless support.

—ISABELLA GINANNESCHI

I wish to thank all the home-owners, major and minor, foreign and local, who so unselfishly, and unwittingly, allowed me into their lives. May you all prosper to give something back to beautiful Bali. Special thanks to my tireless editors at Abbeville, Jackie Decter and Abigail Asher, who so graciously queried the dirty bits and let the fun bits pass.

— MADE WIJAYA

EDITORS: Abigail Asher, Jacqueline Decter
DESIGNER: Patricia Fabricant
MAP: Sophie Kittredge
PRODUCTION DIRECTOR: Louise Kurtz

Photographs copyright © 2000 Isabella Ginanneschi. Text and compilation, including selection of text and images, copyright © 2000 Abbeville Press. All rights reserved under international copyright conventions. No part of this book may be reproduced or utilized in any form or by any means, electronic or mechanical, including photocopying, recording, or by any information storage and retrieval system, without permission in writing from the publisher. Inquiries should be addressed to Abbeville Publishing Group, 22 Cortlandt Street, New York, N.Y. 10007. The text of this book was set in Adobe Garamond and Felix Titling. Printed and bound in Hong Kong.

First edition
10 9 8 7 6 5 4 3 2 1

Library of Congress Cataloging-in-Publication Data

Wijaya, Made.
At home in Bali / photographs by Isabella Ginanneschi ; text by Made Wijaya.
p. cm.
Includes index.
ISBN 0-7892-0467-3
1. Bali Island (Indonesia)—Description and travel. 2. Bali Island (Indonesia)—Pictorial works. I. Title.

DS647.B2 W499 2000
959.8'6—DC21   99-058475

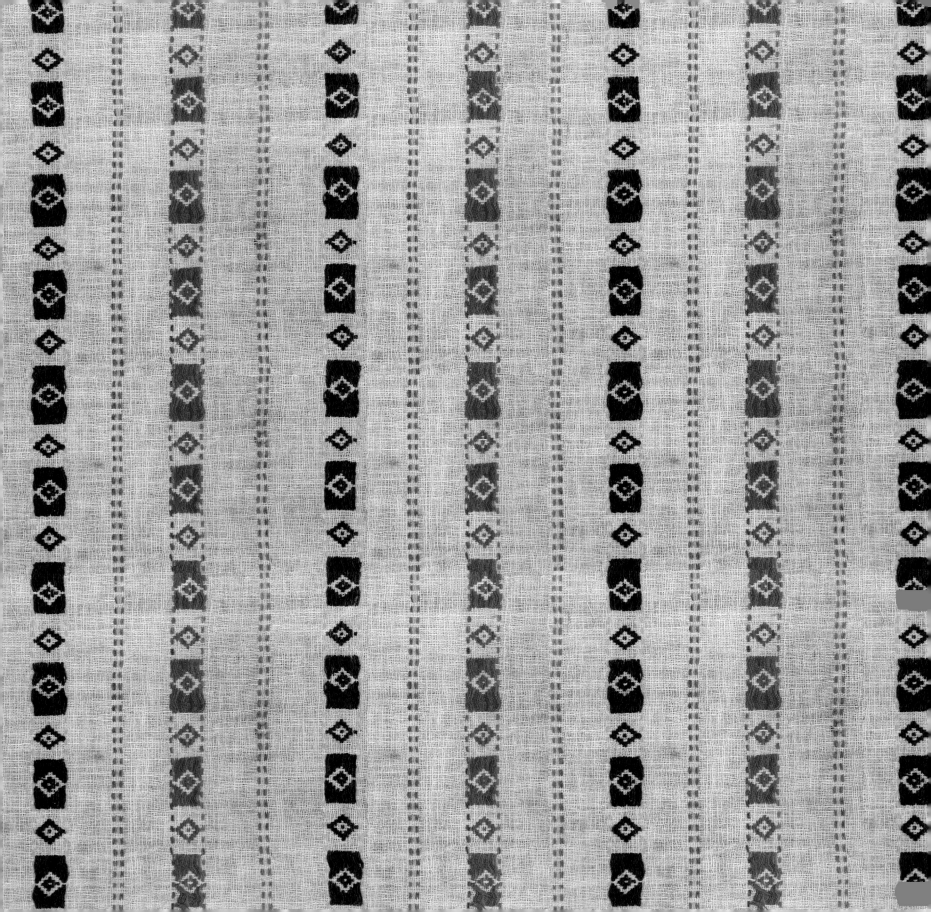